CONTENTS

First, I will like to thank you for taking the first step of trusting me and deciding to purchase/read this life-transforming Book. Thanks for spending your time and resources on this material.

I can assure you of exact results if you will diligently follow the exact blueprint, I lay bare in the information manual you are currently reading. It has transformed lives, and I strongly believe it will equally transform your own life too.

All the information I presented in this Do It Yourself piece is easy to digest and practice.

INTRODUCTION

If you want peace, peace is already there. If you want joy, love, harmony, understanding, wisdom, and happiness—these, too, are already present, right in the nature of things. You do not need to travel to Tibet or India. You do not need to find the perfect teacher or the perfect retreat. You do not have to do anything special whatsoever. All you need to do is open yourself gently to receive what already is, as the earth receives the rain, as a flower opens to the sun. Perhaps the most painful and damaging illusion of all is the notion that peace and happiness are to be found in the future. When we finish that degree or find the right job or the right relationship, then, we believe, we will be happy. And these may in fact be good things. But peace and happiness can only be now. If we can touch peace and happiness in this moment, future moments will also contain peace and happiness. If we cannot touch peace and happiness now, when will we? Practically speaking, however, we are prone to lose our way. Both spiritual and psychological practice are a kind of medicine to help us find the means to recontact peace when we no longer seem to know how. In Part I, we describe the nature of the problems we face in the modern world, and how mindfulness or holding to the center can help. Today many of us see life as a problem to be solved rather than an experience to be lived, looking everywhere but within, everywhere but at our own experiencing. We suffer from fragmentation, disconnection, negative emotions, and low self-esteem. We burden our primary relationships with impossible expectations, and live for the never-arriving future. Mindfulness, on the other hand, centers us in our own lives, empowering us to find our own internal authority. Mindfulness is deeply connected also to the practice of no self, which we introduce in this section.

KNOW WHERE YOU BELONG AND WHERE YOU ARE

The basic thing individuals need to know from educators and specialists comes down to this: How would I be able to be glad? How might I discover harmony?

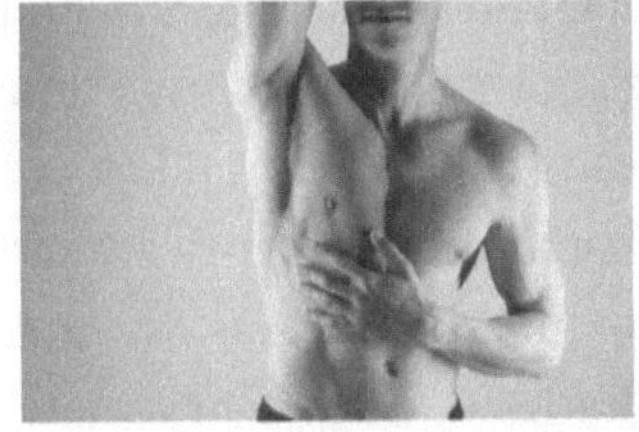

The fundamental answer is consistently the equivalent: Begin where you are. Once the 1970s were the "Me Decade," and the 1980s were the time of insatiability, today we think back on an era of developing self-distraction. Freud distributed his first significant work, The Interpretation of Dreams, directly at the introduction of the twentieth century. Furthermore, starting there on, we have been progressively intrigued with ourselves. However simultaneously, our uneasiness and vulnerability have just expanded. For this interest and distraction, we are more alienated than any other time in recent memory from ourselves and our reality. The reasons we have neglected to discover harmony through such a lot of surprising exertion are certainly unpredictable. Yet, some portion of the appropriate response is that we are looking in an inappropriate spot.

Some portion of the appropriate response is that the majority of our looking through turns into dead end in the event that it is established in a key doubt of ourselves and our inclination. Brain science can help and otherworldliness can help. In any case, as long as our looking is established in self-doubt, we will consistently be taking a stab at another person's answer. Workshops and retreats and different instruments must be useful once you use them to enable you to associate with where you are.

There are a wide range of difficulties, jobs, and barriers in our lives that add to pushing the stone tough. There are additionally numerous dispositions and convictions that add to our ceaseless movement that leads us no place and in certainty keeps us stuck in a similar spot. Be that as it may, before attempting to comprehend the exit plan, we have to investigate how we got into this wreckage in any case. Take a gander at Life's Curveballs Sometimes life tosses a significant curve-ball at us. Times of significant change, for good or sick, are clear difficulties to our ability to stay focused. At such occasions, even the most profoundly progressed and mentally entire among us will be misled.

Among the negative changes, there are the conspicuous horrible mishaps, for example, the demise of a companion, parent, kid, or other cherished one; the sudden and undesired separation; the signifi-cant medical issue. These are troublesome sections, requiring time, tolerance, and a ton of help from others. We are tossed out of cadence and equalization. What's more, in reality it would be unusual and unnatural if passing or significant misfortune didn't influence us profoundly. For a period, life is vacant and trivial. Be that as it may, over the long haul, we continue our lives and go on. As we travel through our anguish, we start to mend and slowly we can come back to focus. In the long run we incorporate the misfortune and capacity once more, however we stay changed by the experience. Less by and large recognized is that positive changes, for example, advancements, marriage, profession changes, graduations, critical achievement, and the introduction of youngsters, are additionally troublesome curveballs. While we may feel unbelievably glad, the earth is moving underneath our feet, and it very well may be hard to remain focused and serene. Thus even despite favorable luck, we may lose our middle. Life's curveballs, while troublesome, are regardless open doors for learning and development to happen. Life is a school and the universe is always sending us exercises. In any case, we need an approach to return to the inside with the goal that we can take a gander at the destruction that these occasions can unleash on our psychospiritual prosperity, get them, and proceed on our way. Yet, maybe much increasingly significant are the foundation strains, the constant states of present day life that make it hard to remain focused during times of significant change.

OPEN TO ABUNDANCE

So for what reason do we lose our direction in any event, when there are no significant misfortunes or changes? What thumps us off base and keeps us from clutching that fair, quiet spot: the middle inside? In Buddhist cosmology there is an unusual and impossible to miss domain called the place where there is eager apparitions. The place where there is eager apparitions floods, as the Bible would put it, with milk and nectar. It is a place where there is wealth. The creatures that abide there, be that as it may, are somewhat abnormal. They have colossal, vacant, enlarged midsections and modest, stick size openings for mouths. This is an image, as such, of a tremendous craving, however a powerlessness to fulfill it regardless of how plentiful the encompassing scene. Truth be told, the horrendous part of this domain isn't that anything is missing, but instead, that everything is there, directly before you, promptly and effectively accessible. No one but you can't profit yourself of it since you can never get enough of it through your small mouth. It isn't need, yet the powerlessness to open to the encompassing bounty that is the wellspring of the torment. Somehow or another the created countries of the West are simply such a domain.

We live in a land flooding and bottomless, yet we are tormented by nervousness, wretchedness, and disappointment. Rather than getting a charge out of the plenitude, we center around what is inadequate. Like hungry phantoms, we never get enough. The plenitude just persuades us that we are not getting our offer, expanding our effectively swollen cravings. Regardless of the amount we have, the attention stays on having more. The fact of the matter isn't so a lot of that craving isn't right in essence. You are not a realist for needing bounty or a careerist for craving achievement. The universe is liberal and aches to favor you with your profound longing. Yet, these things can wind up hazardous when we put them at the inside. Want can prompt an unending cycle. While we envision a specific degree of riches will do the trick, once accomplished, this level is never again very enough. We at that point need still somewhat more. The endeavor to discover harmony by such means is an endeavor to extinguish our thirst with saltwater: the very idea of our endeavors just exacerbates it.

Departure from the Future Another explanation we lose our inside is that we delay life instead of live it. Arranging is unavoidable somewhat, and arranging is no more the adversary than want is. In any case, when making arrangements for the future assumes control over the present to such a degree, that the present ends up incredible, meager, and ghostlike, we have lost our middle. Arranging carefully means realizing we are simply arranging. We don't mistake it for the present reality. At the point when done in the correct soul, there's a softness about arranging. You realize the truth is interminably intricate and unendingly developing past our ability to anticipate. Also, since our arrangements consequently need ceaseless refining and modification—if not add up to correction—there is no sense to get excessively got up to speed in them. Would you be able to appreciate future nourishment? Would you be able to drink tomorrow's water? The vast majority of us attempt to do only that, yet you can just sustain yourself with the nourishment and water that are at this very moment. The understudy delays life till he gets his degree, the specialist till she accomplishes some envisioned tallness of budgetary achievement. Is that individual out going around the track genuinely upbeat? Maybe not. His head might be loaded up with dreams of what he will resemble a half year from now, when he can run more distant and quicker, when his muscle to fat ratio is even lower. What's more, in the in the interim, we all are missing it. We are feeling the loss of our lives. The incongruity is, an actual existence brimming with purported reason and arranging and objectives is eventually without point. For while we are distracted with our arrangements, life is going on. Life isn't holding up until we are finished arranging. And keeping in mind that we are characterizing our objectives, we are feeling the loss of the entire thing. Forever comprises just of this present minute —the one we are so bustling fleeing from.

Become Aware of Fragmentation An extraordinary issue of present-day life that takes away from our prosperity is the fracture we experience as we are squeezed between clashing jobs and undertakings. The numerous veils we wear and the jobs we play can lead us away from the middle. Our work can be dividing, and it doesn't make a difference how muddled the activity is. Here and there other individuals' work looks unbelievably simpler than our own. Yet, when you're in that evidently basic activity, despite everything it has numerous angles and requests. Being a homemaker, for instance, isn't the straightforward assignment others impractically envision: "What is most significant for me to do now? Would it be advisable for me to do the shopping for food or go to the cleaner's? Do the banking or vacuum the rug? Have I done what's needed currently to have the option to take a break and accomplish something I appreciate, such as viewing my preferred program, perusing my book, tuning in to my preferred orchestra, or simply calling a companion and talking for some time? Or on the other hand do I have to accomplish all the more first?

Furthermore, gracious, I neglected to defrost something for supper today around evening time." And exactly when you think you have it made sense of, the children get back home from school and request your consideration; the telephone rings and that forceful long separation transporter attempts once more to sell you its administrations (how did you ever jump on its rundown, in any case?); the doorbell rings; you abruptly recall you have to pay the home loan. There is not much or straightforward about running a home. Indeed, even inside this one job, there are many contending requests. What's more, obviously it is more muddled than this for huge numbers of us.

A large portion of us must arrangement with the multifaceted nature of one job, however with adjusting the intricacy of numerous jobs. Is anyone surprised that we now and again wind up longing for some other, less complex time; some past or future Eden; some time when we realize what is anticipated from us; some time when things are simpler; some time when we can simply win a living, or simply be a homemaker, or simply be a parent or a companion or a life partner; or some time when we don't need to do any of that whatsoever and can simply sit on the sea shore and taste margaritas? Beverly says, we should move to the islands and sell T-shirts. However she realizes this is the time we have, the existence we have.

Recognize Your Many Roles Get out pen and book. Sit unobtrusively for a couple of minutes, breathing tenderly. Begin to think about the numerous jobs and parts of your life. Rundown every one of the jobs that you play. Obviously, you may think first about your job at work— the primary thing we're asked at gatherings and get-togethers. In any case, that one job has numerous subroles. For instance, in case you're a lawyer, you might be part advisor, part litigator, part on-screen character, part specialist, part agent, etc. Likewise incorporate the jobs that you play as spouse or wife, parent, child or little girl, etc. Make your rundown as far as might be feasible, thinking of in any event twenty-five jobs or somewhere in the vicinity, considering even viewpoints that are very little, for example, salon client or mail beneficiary. At the point when you have recorded the same number of jobs as you can, read your rundown over reflectively. Presently ask yourself delicately and over and over: Who am I? without attempting to respond to the inquiry, simply holding it in your mindfulness for a couple of minutes.

Disengagement and division from our groups of starting point and companions, combined with occasional change in geographic areas, all signify lost focus. There are many symptoms to disengagement from loved ones. What's more, once in a while these reactions occupy us from our feeling of equalization and harmony and cause us to lose our direction. For the vast majority of mankind's history, individuals didn't wander past a sweep of a couple of miles. Our bodies and sensory systems are the same as our predecessors who experienced their peaceful, nearby lives. Most individuals personally knew where they were conceived, and knew a similar arrangement of relatives and neighbors their entire lives. For us, it is impossibly extraordinary. We barely know where we live.

Our vehicles whisk us past them too rapidly. We don't have a town, not by any means an area. And afterward at regular intervals or somewhere in the vicinity, we move and start once more. Deep rooted companions are uncommon. What we have are companions from various sections in our lives. Also, most of these blur into the past as we move to new places and occupations. Regardless of whether we prefer living as such or not, our Stone Age bodies and cerebrums are sick prepared for it. There is a steady foundation worry to lives so detached from the underlying foundations of spot and network. At that point when life tosses us a significant curveball, it is no big surprise we do not have the assets to adapt to it. Be that as it may, this is just the well-known piece. This is the piece we as a whole discussion about. There is significantly more. Separation runs further.

RECONNECTING WITH YOUR ORIGIN

Invest some energy considering the individuals who have been imperative to you. Make certain to consider all the various occasions and places of your life. Presently record the names of the critical individuals you have put some distance between. For every one on your rundown, consider the conditions under which you lost contact. Is it accurate to say that it was simply floating separated as one of you moved away? Or on the other hand was your separation the aftereffect of some cognizant decision, in view of difference? Or on the other hand would it say it was maybe indistinct how you floated separated? Notice any examples. Attempt to see past accusing it is possible that them or yourself. At that point for every individual on the rundown, think about whether you should restore contact here and there.

Structure an arrangement to recontact anybody you may get a kick out of the chance to. There will be a few people you will most likely be unable to contact since you never again realize how to discover them, and other people who, for some explanation, you judge it best not to be in contact with by any means. That is alright. Such decisions must be made in opportunity and not constrained. For those you would prefer not to contact or can't contact, put in almost no time picturing them. Consider them to be glad, grinning, and satisfied. Once you have awful emotions about them, discharge them by advising yourself that, whatever they did to hurt you, they were simply attempting to be cheerful and abstain from enduring as per their best understanding around then. Don't simply say the words, however give a valiant effort to give this a chance to be a profound goal.

Know about Self-Punishing Thoughts Spend a day rehearsing consciousness of your inclination to participate in self-critical, negative reasoning. Mark each example you notice and number them successively: "Self-misuse number 1, self-misuse number 2, . . . self-misuse number 37, etc. Once you lose tally, simply start at one once more. Do this in a carefree manner. Snicker. In the event that you do this profoundly, you will see that numerous musings may contain an understood self-basic component as opposed to an immediate analysis of yourself. Check these moreover. Once you have a great deal of these contemplations, you may get a kick out of the chance to proceed with this training for a few days. Check whether, by the procedure of mindfulness and without attempting to address the contemplations, they naturally start to diminish. Mindfulness itself is mending.

BECOME THE BELOVED PERSON

With book and pen before you, think about the individual you feel nearest to—maybe your accomplice in the event that you have one, maybe a companion or connection if not. With eyes shut, envision yourself turning into that individual. Be him physically. Think his contemplations. Feel his sentiments. Presently open your eyes. Give this individual a chance to express his most profound emotions, his expectations and fears, his qualities and self-question, everything. Additionally record this present individual's emotions about you. Record this all. Try not to stress whether this is exact or not. Truth be told, don't expect that it is. It isn't the specific things that are of significance, yet attempting to see it from the other's perspective. Thusly, you may start to see whether your estimates are right, since you start to watch all the more intently. Maybe you even inquire. It is tied in with focusing.

Wearing unique garments contains control. I knew a pastor who wore an administrative neckline consistently. At a certain point he thought about leaving the congregation, yet at last he chose to remain. What held him was a straightforward idea: He couldn't envision not putting on his neckline toward the beginning of the day. At the point when a conventional Buddhist priest or sister wakes in the first part of the day, there are no decisions to be made about what to wear. Each morning, he puts on his robe. Each morning, she puts on her shoes. Each morning, he takes his bowl to ask nourishment for the afternoon. Each time you put on your garments in the first part of the day this week, or change them during the day, or take them off around evening time, say to yourself, "This is my robe, these are my shoes." Whenever you take out your wallet to pay for something, state to yourself, "This is my asking bowl that the universe has filled." Use this as an approach to advise yourself that, whatever job that you might play right now, your focal calling is equivalent to that of anybody compelled: to be an individual of harmony, of quiet, of care, of lovingkindness and sympathy, of bliss, and of serenity. This is your actual vocation.

DISCOVER A PATH TO THE CENTER

In the prompt understanding of the Presence, the Now is no insignificant nodal point between the past and what's to come. It is the seat and area of the Divine Presence itself. Never again is the strip [of time] spread out with equivalent striking quality before one, for the past issues less and the future issues less, for the Now contains all that is required for the supreme fulfillment of our most profound yearnings.

Harmony can be tricky. Once you look for it yet neglect to discover it, the issue isn't generally absence of exertion. Some of the time you are looking in an inappropriate spot. In the event that the issue is something ailing in you that should be filled all things considered, at that point whatever encounters you look for will just baffle you. You are left in the domain of over expectation, fracture, and disengagement. You end up in the place that is known for the ravenous apparitions, where you stay unfilled and unsatisfied notwithstanding the bounty surrounding you. Obviously, once you come up short on the necessities of nourishment, safe house, and apparel, it is hard to discover harmony. In addition, once you need more achievement and gratefulness, once you need an accomplice, or if absence of cash keeps you from getting a charge out of a significant number of the beneficial things throughout everyday life, these are significant, as well. It is a misstep to be otherworldly to the point that you don't respect such needs.

Be that as it may, if harmony means having every one of our needs met in an absolutely acceptable manner, we will never discover it. For the greater part of us, our disappointment isn't tied in with satisfying essential needs. It is about interminably looking outside of ourselves and our own understanding for what was never absent in any case.

We don't have to fill ourselves with new things—we have to encounter all the more completely what is now there. So how would we figure out how to mellow and open to what is now present? How would we come to live completely and profoundly this life and not some envisioned life that we trust some time or another to have? In this section we depict the primary rule for finding the inside, the Buddhist routine with regards to care, and show how it meets the situations of current life.

CARE

Care is a nature of delicate nearness. Care is the ability to be available with what is happening at this very moment, without judgment or opposition, without avoidance or investigation. It is a readiness to encounter without reservation what's going on in our embraces current circumstances. It is the act of radical acknowledgment. This is more obvious as an idea than it is to experience or practice. In any case, the training is what is important. Frequently we despise what's going on in the present. This is the reason we keep so caught up with, attempting to propel ourselves ahead to some future time when things will be arranged more the manner in which we like, taking part in all way of imagination about how it will be in that fanciful future. It really is great that life doesn't come furnished with a quick forward catch.

We would all be dead as of now. For as opposed to encountering what is happening, we are caught up with attempting to maintain a strategic distance from it. In any event, when we attempt to come into the present minute in a careful manner, a large portion of us experience the wild, obstinate nature of the psyche. This "monkey mind" is a complete anxiety and bouncing about from appendage to appendage and tree to tree, never halting anyplace for extremely long, not completing this chomp of our banana before we are as of now stuffing the following one in. Luckily, there is help. There are tried and true approaches to create more prominent nearness or care in your life. There are approaches to figure out how to keep your meeting with life in the main spot it tends to be kept:

· · ·

the present minute. That is the uplifting news. What's more, we will acquaint you with a portion of these ways, both Eastern and Western, both antiquated and present day.

THREE KINDS OF EXPERIENCES: WORKING WITH THEM EFFECTIVELY

Though care is a solitary thing, it is useful to recognize three sorts of books: things that are troublesome and excruciating; things that are brilliant, mending, and reestablishing; and things that are some place in the middle of or impartial. The act of care includes these. Once you are doing strolling contemplation along a woods way and all of a sudden recall that there isn't sufficient cash in your financial balance to cover a check you composed before that day, you ought to know that you are strolling down the timberland way. Return to the present. Feel the earth underneath your feet. Smell the pine trees. Feel the breeze touch your hair. Notice the little wildflowers at the edge of the way. Be the place you are.

This is the act of being in contact with what is mending and reestablishing. This doesn't imply that you should attempt to curb your monetary dread. You need to regard these emotions and work with them. However, remember to experience strolling in the back-woods when you are strolling in the timberland. Some dread or stress or concern is continually lying in hang tight for us. What is the purpose of being alive by any stretch of the imagination, once we let these things rule our consideration? This is developing care of what is great. The second sort of training is to work with the negative incli-nation itself—for this situation, the budgetary dread. Notwithstanding, and still, after all that, you should be in contact with the present minute. To rehearse along these lines is as a result to let yourself know: "Here I am strolling in the timberland, and further-more stressing over my financial records. I hold these sentiments of dread softly, and grin at them. I am totally ready to be here, strolling in the woods, and furthermore having these musings and fears about cash." With delicate constancy, you realize what your dread is attempting to show you and coordinate it, however are never again hostage to it. You may even have the option to return to simply strolling in the backwoods. This in itself is a wonder. Development has given us a gastrointestinal framework that is capable at processing the nourishment and supplements we have to keep up a solid body.

IT ISN'T CONSTANTLY IMPECCABLE.

A few people have hypersensitivities to specific nourishments. These kinds of nourishment won't be processed well and may cause issues. We all lose stomach related catalysts as we age. Nourishment that we once could process effectively now never again concurs with us. Numerous individuals, for instance, lose the capacity to process dairy items. So also, the human personality is the endowment of development too. It has turned out to be adroit at foreseeing issues and settling them. It has turned out to be great at processing unpalatable encounters. Disturbing encounters might be used in dreams, or by pondering them until we are through reasoning and discussing them. In some cases, be that as it may, this arrangement of mental absorption separates. Here and there the brain stalls out in its handling. We may have intermittent dreams, or even remember horrendous encounters as though they are going on once more. Somebody with post-awful pressure issue (PTSD) may remember wartime encounters over and over, trapped in an unending and startling circle. At the point when we get trapped in such a circle, when our psyches are not processing troublesome emotions and encounters, we need assistance. Now we need some approach to carry serenity to our experience. Similarly as we don't process appropriately in the event that we eat while we are disturbed, so we can't process emotions once we are not quiet. Once we can't do this all alone, psychotherapy intends to reestablish our capacity to process troublesome encounters, so we can gain from them without being overwhelmed by them. Key in this procedure is the capacity to perceive that what you are encountering is a memory and not a present reality.

The nearness of a specialist

enables customers to understand that they are not remembering this old experience, however they are sheltered with a minding individual next to them, recollecting that it. At the point when this occurs, the mind's ability to process the troublesome experience is reestablished. We stall out when fears, stresses, or old injuries put us into a stupor of torment that removes us from the present minute. So with the individual strolling in the woods and agonizing over cash, it is significant that he realizes he is strolling in the backwoods. Once he gets so got up to speed in his dread that he is overwhelmed by it, with similar musings and sentiments circling interminably, he will stall out there. It is as of now supportive when he understands that he is in an exquisite woodland, strolling in harmony, even while simultaneously he has this dread and stress. That way, he isn't totally inundated in the negative material. Nonpartisan encounters can end up positive in the event that we get them with smoothness and lucidity. The bluebird that flew right over our way at the beginning of today as Beverly and I went for our morning stroll was excellent.

Be that as it may, if our brains were unsettled, we may have encountered it as unbiased or not have seen it by any stretch of the imagination. Wouldn't that have been a disgrace? Also, drinking a glass of water might be unbiased, however once you experience it completely, it tends to be a delight. The breath is frequently experienced as nonpartisan, however it very well may be very charming once we offer thoughtfulness regarding it. Breath additionally can enable us to quiet down and process negative encounters, change nonpartisan occasions into positive ones, and decrease our experiencing negative encounters. Tally the Breath Sit serenely. Relax any tight dress. Give your mind a chance to move in the direction of your relaxing. With the first in-breath, tally one. With the first outbreath, check one. With the second in-breath, check two, and with the second out-breath, tally two, proceeding up to ten. At the point when your mind meanders, return to the breathing, and start again with one. At the point when you arrive at ten, return to one. Proceed for five to ten minutes. Practice in a nice, loosening up way. At the point when you are prepared to stop, delay for one more moment, and feel the impact of having done this on your body and brain.

Contemplation, for instance, is tied in with figuring out how to be increasingly careful, about coming into your real life and experience, about getting a charge out of the present minute. Be that as it may, numerous individuals transform contemplation into a venture. As a venture, reflection can wind up unbending and objective situated. You fantasize about when you can think so well—when you are edified to such an extent—that life will consistently stream easily and everything will become alright. Or on the other hand more regrettable still, you begin to consider yourself "otherworldly." This turns out to be one more job you play, a picture to satisfy. What's more, in satisfying that picture, you become specifically open to specific encounters and shut to others that you would lean toward not to take note. You may enable yourself to encounter quiet sentiments. In any case, you may oppose seeing that you feel exhausted, in light of the fact that weariness doesn't accommodate your concept of yourself as an otherworldly individual. What's more, it is significantly harder to concede that you are furious. Any instructing, any methodology or strategy, turns into a deterrent once we let it. The Buddha depicted his instructing as resembling a snake.

It must be taken up cautiously, or you will get chomped, and be more awful off than you were previously. You can take any instructing, regardless of how helpful, and make an icon of it, continually checking your experience against it. Furthermore, if your experience doesn't fit, you compel it into the form of what you figure you should understanding. This isn't the way. The path is to be with whatever you are encountering, and to recognize it as authentic, yet even as essential. There is a Zen saying that once you meet the Buddha out and about, murder him. This is a stunning thought. However, the stun dazzles the point. Likewise with strict language when all is said in done, this isn't to be taken inflexibly or truly. What is inferred is that even the Buddha—a completely edified being—can be a risk to you. Once the Buddha turns into a symbol, once you attempt to adjust to your picture of what a Buddha resembles, this ends up dangerous. Truth be told, complying with any picture at all is something contrary to care.

Regardless of whether the picture you are complying with is certain or negative, care is missing at whatever point we attempt to cause our experience to be what we figure it ought to be as opposed to enabling it to be what it is. This battle inside ourselves to have just specific sorts of encounters is the fundamental explanation we need harmony.

TRY NOT TO WORRY ABOUT ACTING THE RIGHT WAY

Some of us harm ourselves by the very force of our endeavors. Our longing to be correct and right meddles with coming into the present minute. In the event that you are even somewhat increasingly present to your life, even somewhat less occupied by musings and stresses and plans, at that point you are doing it right. You are moving the correct way.

RADICAL ACCEPTANCE: THE NEED TO PRACTICE IT

The act of care is a sort of radical acknowledgment. It isn't so a lot of that we try to be serene, regardless of what's going on, as it is that in any event, when we are not quiet, we acknowledge that experience, similarly all things considered. Once along these lines we check out what is, regardless of whether what is something we don't especially need, harmony rises. To put it to some degree in an unexpected way, quite a bit of what meddles with our satisfaction in life is the ceaseless battle to force an alternate sort of request on understanding than what is as of now there. Harmony is discovered when we stop this battle.

Furthermore, the entryway to the discontinuance of battle is first to acknowledge that at the present time, battle is what is happening. Some item now that extreme acknowledgment is risky, that our own experience isn't to be trusted. Yet, by and by, you must choose between limited options. Once you don't acknowledge your own understanding, what else would you be able to do? Regardless of whether you place your confidence in some outside power, it is still you who must choose which authority you will acknowledge. So how would you realize you can confide in your choice? The German rationalist Friedrich Nietzsche talked about human improvement in his well-known illustration of the camel, the lion, and the youngster. From the start, we are the camel.

We have to assume the heap of custom, of standards and rules for our conduct. Once we don't do this in early life, we are not cultivated creatures by any means. Rather, we live in the realm of teeth and paws and savage hostility. In any case, at that point we should make the progress to the lion. Now we come into our capacity. Despite everything we observe the principles, however we use them to accomplish and succeed. We become something on the planet. In any case, at long last, we become the kid, and as the kid, we lose the standards we took on as the camel and come back to honesty and opportunity.

This resembles Saint Augustine's announcement, "Love God, and do what you will." If you do what you will while having the affection for God in your heart, there's no threat of your fouling up. The individual who arrives at the youngster stage is as yet an enlightened being, however the principles and customs never again limit her opportunity.

LOCATING SELF: A MIRROR INTO REALITY

Try this analysis to have an encounter of no self. Sit for a couple of minutes and watch as musings and emotions come into your psyche. Where do they originate from? Where do they go? We accept we think, however in the event that we look all the more carefully, the experience of what we call believing is increasingly similar to considerations simply traveling every which way without anyone else. They show up, expound on themselves, at that point go once more. We are no more accountable for this procedure than we are of mists going through the sky. Presently ask yourself: Where is something which I can call "I"?

All there is only this flood of idea and believing and experience. You can say you are the experiencer, however that is simply one more idea. The Purpose Is to Be Fully Alive At a discussion I gave, somebody questioned the possibility of no self, saying that oneself is what is doing the watching. This is a smart remark, and demonstrates that the individual paid attention to the thought. Be that as it may, what happens when this self-quits watching? Where is it at that point? Once oneself exists just discontinuously, at that point it is something very not the same as what we typically mean when we talk about self. It is impressively less strong and generous. The truth, as indicated by Buddhist lessons, is that self is simply one more idea in the surge of our contemplations.

This may sound somewhat obscure. Be that as it may, this rule is entirely functional. The way to understanding Buddhism is to consider it to be constantly about training, about torment and the finish of affliction. The Buddha was constantly down to earth. Once in a while he would not respond to theoretical otherworldly addresses presented by inquisitive followers—not on the grounds that he proved unable, but since he didn't feel it was useful to get diverted by such things. It might appear to be alarming to address such an essential thought as the presence of a self. It can give you that sentiment of being on no strong ground, as though there's a quake going on. In any case, when you move beyond the underlying stun, it is freeing. Surrender the Chase There's a guard sticker that peruses: "Life is a game.

The one with the most toys at last successes." Funny, yes. Yet additionally tragic. Wins what? Wins the coronary failure? Wins the prize of passing on right on time from one of the numerous different pressure related sicknesses? Wins the prize of missing the entire thing since you are never fully where you are, doing what you're doing, however are continually dashing ahead to the following thing, as though life itself were a race or a challenge? We pay a horrendous cost when we think we are in a self circumstance however are very a no-self circumstance. What's more, we are entirely in a no-self circumstance.

Take another model—a prospective employee meeting. You have looked into this position, and you feel that you need it without question. Since you are considering it a self circumstance, or, in other words a success lose circumstance, you get aggressive. Your heart races and your perspiration organs become overactive.

This thusly makes you reluctant. You re-think yourself always: "Was that the correct answer? Kid, that was inept!" Because of this frame of mind, you are tight and restless, and you don't establish the connection you could make once you were progressively loose. Indeed, even a prospective employee meeting is a no-self circumstance. What great is it to win the position, in the event that you, at that point loathe it, if one month from now you wind up brushing the classifieds once more? In the event that you consider this to be a no-self circumstance, at that point you realize that there is no triumphant for only you except if everybody in this circumstance likewise wins.

Both you and the business must be upbeat, or the outcomes won't be useful for anybody. Once you land the position since you have established an excessively positive false connection, what have you truly prevailing with regards to doing? You have made a circumstance that can just motivation awful sentiments and dissatisfaction for everybody concerned, including yourself. Amusingly, in the event that you see reality of this, you are bound to make a decent impression, since you are increasingly loose and more yourself. The possibility of no self is to encounter reality in an alternate manner, to see our interconnectedness with all things.

It is a method for expelling the cover from our eyes, so we can see that we, such as everything known to mankind, are always showing signs of change, not some strong constant element. Try not to get captured by this as a plan to contend about. It isn't something to guard, nor something to banter against. It is an encounter. It is a method for seeing. So no self isn't obscure. It is down to earth and viable. It works. The act of care is actually this straightforward, minute by-minute consideration. It is serene and reviving to be in that spot: Now this is occurring, presently this is going on, presently this, etc. It turns into a battle when thoughts of self downer in: "Am I doing it right? Am I being careful enough? Kid, I'm not generally excellent at this!" Noticing the contrast between these two sorts of mindfulness is itself the exit plan. Yet, progressively about that later.

TEA MEDITATION: THE BEST TAKE TO HAVE BREAK AND COMFORTABLE LEISURE.

Maybe give yourself some tea or a bit of natural product to appreciate, or whatever your body might want at the present time. Set up your tea or nibble in a casual manner, mindful of every development. Give it a chance to resemble opening a Christmas present: Instead of doing it in a rushed and unseemly manner, take as much time as necessary with it, getting a charge out of the entire procedure. Setting up your tea is as substantial as drinking it. Remain right now. At the point when your musings advance beyond you, tenderly come back to the present and to what you are doing. Before you start to eat or to drink your tea, delay. Welcome the possibility of your tea or nourishment. At that point gradually start to eat or drink. While tasting or eating, appreciate each taste, smell, and sensation. Notice what it resembles to bite, taste, and swallow. At the point when different concerns emerge, recognize them, and remind yourself you can manage them later. At this moment, just some tea, this bit of natural product, exists. Give yourself the endowment of being right now.

SNAPSHOTS OF MINDFULNESS

There are numerous open doors during the day when we are occupied with a generally straightforward errand that we more often than not do on programmed. For instance: doing the dishes, cleaning up, vacuuming, setting off to the washroom, drinking a glass of water, strolling from your vehicle to the workplace or the store, getting dressed, holding up at a red light, etc. Pick one of these exercises, and in the coming week, take steps to do it with all out care, taking in and out, mindful of what you are doing, not losing all sense of direction in your arrangements and stresses. At the point when your mind meanders, take it back to the present without squandering any vitality in self-recrimination.

How at that point would we say we are to open the entryway of care, and use it in our day by day life? In the event that contemplation is the appropriate response, it has been exhibited in manners that cause it to appear to be overwhelming and hard to most Westerners—a training for the otherworldly Olympians among us. Be that as it may, when the embodiment of reflection is comprehended, this need not be the situation. Furthermore, when we can remove contemplation from our reflection room and into day by day life, a peaceful power develops that, while from the start too inconspicuous to even think about noticing, progressively changes each minute and each experience. Part II is drawn principally from conventional otherworldly practices. In this area, we show you the proper routine with regards to contemplation (weeks three and four). We disclose to you what reflection is and how to do it, and we answer questions with respect to basic troubles.

Mental sources help us comprehend the impacts of reflection and show us how to give ourselves empowering messages. In the parts for quite a long time five and six we tell you the best way to start to incorporate the reflective disposition into every day life. Otherworldly sources are again enhanced with mental info, for example, contrasting careful living and the brain research of "stream," and keeping a fair way of life.

A MILD APPROACH TOWARDS MEDITATION THAT WORKS

We as of now are what we need to turn into. We don't need to progress toward becoming another person. We should simply act naturally, completely and legitimately. We don't need to pursue anything. We as of now contain the entire universe. We just come back to ourselves through care and contact the harmony and bliss that are as of now present inside us and surrounding us. I have shown up. I am home. There is nothing to do.

THE ATTITUDE IN MEDITATION

There is no better strategy for profound change and finding internal harmony than contemplation. Mental research, for example, that directed by the Harvard specialist Herbert Benson has itemized the significant physiological impacts of contemplation. At the point when we think, our heartbeat backs off and our pulse drops. Our mind movement shifts toward alpha waves—mirroring a condition of quiet mindfulness. These progressions immunize us against many pressure related sicknesses, and they happen in even amateur meditators. However these physiological changes scarcely address the difference in awareness that best in class meditators report. For reflection isn't only for adjusting the body and the brain (which it does), it is a way of edification, an approach to come into that spot of unfaltering harmony called nirvana, moksha, satori—the kingdom of paradise. Be that as it may, the act of contemplation is loaded with mystery.

Attempting to discover harmony, we first experience uneasiness. Attempting to simply be, we experience the wild hecticness of our psyches, unendingly stressing, envisioning, arranging, or lamenting. This underlying background makes a few of us pull back from contemplation, happy to come back to the interruption of our bustling lives. Is it feasible for conventional individuals—who are neither holy people nor religious zealots, not priests, nuns, or masters —to move toward becoming meditators and to utilize this technique for harmony and change for themselves? Completely. The main catch is that despite the fact that you begin to ruminate for an explanation— regardless of whether it's to arrive at edification or just to vaccinate yourself against stress—you should surrender this very objective, permitting your reflection practice to unfurl as though you were not looking to achieve anything by any stretch of the imagination.

Contemplation Is a Natural State Meditation is regular. Similarly as you don't need to work to see the shading blue or hear the sound of traffic passing by, you don't have to attempt to compel yourself to achieve anything extraordinary so as to think. Empowering reflective mindfulness is similar to empowering rest. You can get things done to encourage rest: holding on to hit the sack until you feel sluggish; killing splendid lights and placing yourself in an agreeable, safe, and calm spot; evading caffeine or animating exercises before you hit the hay, etc. Be that as it may, you can't power rest. You can't get rest going. Resting isn't something achieved with resolution and utilized muscles and sewed temples.

Actually, the craft of nodding off is the specialty of escaping your own specific manner enough to enable rest to happen. As everybody who has been up in the center of the night knows, the more you stress over how tired you will be the following day, the more you imagine that you must get the chance to rest at this moment, the more rest evades you. Contemplation is a condition of quiet, ready consideration instead of rest. In any case, likewise with rest, it must be energized and not constrained. In the event that you sit with a frame of mind of achieving or constraining, you immediately come to perceive that you can't control this procedure.

The more you attempt to constrain yourself to feel serene and not feel pitiful or on edge, the less quiet you become. Reflection is the specialty of escaping your own specific manner and of giving the procedure a chance to unfurl at its own pace and beat. It is the easiest thing of all. In any case, we are so used to doing—to being involved and engaged—that it requires a significant stretch of time to re-teach this limit with respect to being. What makes it conceivable in any case is that we are as of now Buddha. We are doing whatever it takes not to compel ourselves to be something unfriendly to our temperament: We are simply revealing what we as of now are, permitting something tremendous and incredible however typically out of sight to come into the forefront of mindfulness.

Contemplation is somewhat similar to what happens when you sit before a pit fire in a tranquil, wonderful spot. It is increasingly centered, yet like your open air fire dream, you are doing whatever it takes not to achieve anything. You are not taking a gander at the fire since it is beneficial for you, or to make quiet sentiments. You are simply taking a gander at the fire. Also, as you take a gander at the fire, your mind settles down without anyone else. As your psyche bit by bit calms down, you draw nearer, layer by layer, to your fundamental Buddha nature. Furthermore, these are not void words. Your Buddha nature is there.

THREE MINDS: A CLOSER LOOK

The purpose behind this report is to enable you to comprehend the connection between your Three Minds by clarifying what they are and how they serve you and how to speak with each of them three. This happened because of my work with a

Ho'o Pono reflection and the acknowledgment that you are increasingly well-suited to utilize the contemplation once you better see how and why it fills in just as it does.

Ho'o Pono is a ground-breaking, life-changing reflection. To get the most profit by the contemplation it sees how it functions and why. It works paying little mind to whether you totally see how and why or not; in any case, I trust it will be substantially more dominant and liberating for you once you can comprehend the how and the why. Understanding the how and why comes because of knowing how your Three Minds work; your Conscious, Unconscious, and Super Conscious Minds - additionally some of the time alluded to as your Three Selves; Lower, Middle, and Higher Self.

You initially should comprehend that everything in your life is 100% your own obligation. This is some of the time hard for some individuals to understand; due in a huge part due to your pasts and your condition, as it were the way society nearly has you prepared or mentally programmed into imagining that you can make someone else feel a specific way. The principal thing you have to comprehend is that you are answerable for your very own emotions, every one of them, and nobody else can make you feel anything. You choose to feel whatever you feel; consistently, without any special cases. I know, I know, this isn't anything but difficult to acknowledge for many individuals, yet it is valid and the sooner you get it, acknowledge it, and start to rehearse it, the sooner you will be free from inclination constrained by any other person.

Once you consider this, I trust you will immediately go to the acknowledgment that it is valid - you dislike it, in any case, it is valid. OK, since you realize that you are answerable for everything that occurs in your life, I despise doing this to you, however it is extremely significant that you additionally comprehend and consider what I am going to state. In addition to the fact that you are liable for everything that goes alone life, you are additionally 100% answerable for anything or potentially all that you hear/see/read about. As it were, once you are conversing with a companion and they inform you regarding something "awful" that transpired they know, presently, you are answerable for that also, whatever it is.

In this way, in addition to the fact that it is hard to grasp being 100% liable for all that you do or say yourself, presently it is practically difficult to understand being answerable for something you knew nothing around 5 minutes prior, however since you think about it, you are liable for it!

I know, I know - in addition to the fact that it is difficult to comprehend or grasp; it is likewise, at the surface, disrupting no doubt. How on earth would that be able to be? All things considered, as a matter of first importance it isn't "on Earth", it is in the Spiritual or oblivious domain.

To enable you to comprehend this better, we should investigate our brains.

For us all "being in agreement", I will ask that you track with me as I clarify how this functions - and the cool part is that once you comprehend this idea, you will at that point see how you can be liable for something you had no part in - or so you thought. Furthermore, why and how Ho'o Pono fills in just as it does.

THE THREE MINDS

Be sure that the three personalities are the Conscious, Unconscious, and Super-Conscious Minds. Otherwise called Body, Mind, and Spirit; Body, Mind, and Soul; Body, Mind, and Emotions; and so on.

· · ·

For this book I will utilize the accompanying:

•The Conscious Mind; at times alluded to as the fantasy of "I".

•The Unconscious Mind, many allude to this as the Sub-cognizant; for this book they mean the equivalent.

•The Super Conscious Mind, otherwise called our Higher Self.

Your Conscious Mind is that piece of you that directions as well as controls your reaction and responses to outer occasions. This is the piece of you that regularly needs to be "Correct". Assume for instance that you approach somebody for assistance with a venture you are dealing with. You have a friendly exchange and exchange thoughts and proposals and land at a settled upon result. At the point when you are done, you feel like everything is ok and complete and in control, in charge.

Presently, we should change that situation a piece and you are having a similar talk, notwithstanding, the other individual proposes thoughts that you don't concur with. They basically decline to see things the manner in which you see them and you can't go to a genial understanding. You begin to have sentiments of disappointment and perhaps outrage begins to emerge. You get yourself 'getting stirred up,' you are not as quiet as when you began. The levelheaded considerations you would regularly have under the past conditions are currently upset by clashing emotions and even thoughts of retribution - you begin to think about things being said literally, begin to speak more loudly and maybe even hurl your arms tragically - basically in light of the fact that the other individual didn't concur with you and what you needed to do.

What occurred, where did these sentiments originate from? They originate from the Unconscious Mind. When these emotions begin to happen, your Conscious Mind starts sending considerations to "Be cool", don't get irritated; keep up your quiet. Your Conscious Mind may likewise be revealing to you that instead of hazard harm to the fellowship, you should be full grown about it and just keep your cool. Your real reaction to the circumstance will be reliant upon your degree of preparing and routine with regards to control the Conscious Mind has over your Unconscious Mind, at the end of the day how well you can control your feelings. This can be troublesome once in a while because of the Unconscious Mind's arrival of adrenaline and the "battle or flight" reaction.

What is the final product of the above situation? In the best of conditions your Conscious Mind will acknowledge what's going on and you won't respond to the negative sentiments raised by your Unconscious Mind; nonetheless, as a general rule, the contrary will happen. You will more than likely express your disappointment with the circumstance or individual helping you just to later lament having had a negative response to the episode. As a rule, after the episode and you have "chilled off", you ask yourself, "What occurred, for what reason did I get so annoyed? I wish I had not responded in such a negative way."

We know about our Conscious Mind, and in specific situations we can see the nearness of our Unconscious Mind. We realize the Conscious Mind gives us our inductive thinking powers, our endowment of discourse and self control. The crucial our Conscious Mind is to deal with the body, to work or acquire a living, to settle on choices and decisions throughout everyday life, and in particular, to guide and advice the Unconscious Mind in its way of development.

. . .

Be that as it may, the Conscious Mind has almost no memory; it can scarcely recollect what you had for breakfast at the beginning of today, and must depend upon the Unconscious Mind for recalling. The Unconscious Mind, then again, remembers everything, it is like a plate drive on your PC in that it stores each snippet of data enabled to it and needs to review any memory whenever. The Unconscious Mind is; be that as it may, the lesser advanced of the three personalities; it has amazing memory capacities, is the seat all things considered, however can't reason. For this, the Unconscious Mind must depend upon the Conscious Mind.

Understand that the Unconscious Mind additionally is effectively naive and exceptionally vulnerable to proposal - this is the reason the "Intensity of Suggestion" ought not be messed with. Curiously enough, this is additionally the wellspring of our mystic capacities and where our capacity to extend, or do astral travel originates from. The Unconscious Mind is additionally the starting point of our instinct.

Presently at that point, all that being said - coming up next is the key segment of the Unconscious Mind. It can fabricate mana vitality - this is the Universal Life Force, otherwise called Chi, or Prana, or on account of Ho'o Pono, Aka. This vitality originates from our condition; the nourishment we eat, the nutrients we take, the air we inhale, and so forth. This vitality isn't vital for the crucial elements of the body, it is likewise essential by the Conscious Mind so as to practice its will and to perform thinking and thinking.

The Unconscious Mind is the place our Aka ropes start. These lines of vitality are anticipated as slender strings of the mystic, imperceptible body and append to other individuals, creatures, or things. These strings convey the mana, the vitality, utilized by the Unconscious

Mind to send data to, or gather it from the outer item. This data is then offered to the Conscious Mind as emotions or natural 'hunches'. The Unconscious Mind is likewise the wellspring of our mending powers. We as a whole can mend; be that as it may, just a couple comprehend and use that capacity.

THE SUPER CONSCIOUS MIND

Be aware that the Super Conscious Mind is in some cases alluded to as our Guardian Angel, the Higher-awareness, or the Master inside. The Ancient Hawaiian Kahunas considered it the aumakua, which signifies, "the absolutely dependable parental soul." The Super Conscious Mind has a prevalent type of reasoning. The Conscious Mind uses thinking and inductive reasoning, the Unconscious Mind utilizes feeling, memory, and feeling, the Super Conscious Mind utilizes a higher type of reasoning that incorporates thinking, feeling, and memory; generally, the Super Conscious Mind is the connection between the Conscious Mind and the Unconscious Mind. The Super Conscious Mind likewise approaches the Universal Knowledge, some of the time known as the Akashic Records. The Akashic Records, be that as it may, is another exchange. For the present, think about the Akashic Records as the Library of the Universe - where all data about everything since the very beginning is put away.

Once and when you have a "Knowing", this originates from the Super Conscious Mind and contacts us such that the thinking of the Conscious Mind doesn't grasp just as the feeling that the Unconscious Mind doesn't fathom. At the point when you get a "Knowing", you can believe that it is for your own advancement.

. . .

Every one of the three Minds are constantly accessible to you consistently; notwithstanding, you can't ordinarily 'hear' the Super Conscious Mind except if you calm the Conscious and Unconscious Minds. Frequently, your Super Conscious Mind is gotten to when you are dozing; you can likewise get to it after supplication, once you stay calm and really 'tune in' for it. Contemplation is the most dependable approach to get to your Super Conscious Mind; this is the reason it is so imperative to learn and rehearse reflection all the time. Most correspondence from the Super Conscious Mind comes to you as Intuition, or an inclination or 'hunch'. Remember that the Super Conscious Mind is that piece of you whose crucial is to control you. Along these lines, it is imperative to figure out how to tune in to what it is letting you know. It is offering you free guidance and will never control you wrong; once you just figure out how to hear it out. Once more, I unequivocally prescribe that you learn and practice reflection all the time.

BLISS

What is the way to joy? The way to joy is learning the structure of your psyches and to start working with them, every one of them three. Through understanding and working with your brains, you can free yourself, or rinse, the majority of your negative contemplations, sentiments, and feelings.

There is expanding medicinal proof that it is the negative musings, sentiments, and feelings that are kept 'caught' inside that is the reason for most, if not all, of the major incessant diseases, both mental and physical. These feelings are the consequence of past occasions that you have 'stuffed', that is have not managed at the hour of event. You keep them caught in your Unconscious Minds where they hold and square a lot of mana vitality. At the point when you don't recognize them suitably, every time something different happens that triggers them, they endeavor to turn out at the same time. This is the reason regularly when something enrages you and you get much more furious than the present condition or circumstance merits, it is on the grounds that that outrage, or negative feeling has opened the Unconscious Mind and everything that is caught inside endeavors to get out, or escape.

In like manner, once you ever feel like you are simply meandering through life capriciously, apparently without reason or significance, it is on the grounds that you have lost the association with your Super Conscious Mind.

Keep in mind, you have three isolated and particular "Personalities", the Conscious, Unconscious, and the Super Conscious Minds. Another approach to see it is that your Unconscious Mind is your creature part, the feelings of which should be restrained and controlled, or oversaw. You have to change the narrow minded, adolescence to participation. Once you don't change your Unconscious Minds and transmute the displeasure, disappointment, hostility, and self-centeredness into adoration, resistance, and empathy, you will keep on riding a crazy ride of turmoil, perplexity, and agony.

The Conscious Mind has the obligation to guide and direction the Unconscious Mind; its strategic to assist the Unconscious Mind with evolving. The Conscious Mind should likewise surrender its conviction that it should be correct and quit controlling the outer world, endeavoring to make it a particular way. The Conscious Mind must wind up gutsy and liberal, unselfish, tolerant, and persistent, just as merciful. To put it plainly, the Conscious Mind must control the negative feelings of the Unconscious Mind. The Super Conscious Mind is with you to guide and advice the lower pair of Minds. It's crucial to assist them with evolving. The three personalities each have various capacities and various needs. You should figure out how to get them to all cooperate utilizing the best capacities of each; the enthusiastic and memory-bound, deductive Unconscious Mind; the objective, coherent and inductive Conscious Mind, and the prevalent cognizance of the Super Conscious Mind. By and by, I can't pressure enough the significance of reflection to unite the Three Minds amicably.

Presently at that point, this is all incredible and magnificent, isn't that so? You comprehend the Three Minds much better; be that as it may, how would you 'come to an obvious conclusion', in a manner of speaking, how would you speak with the Three Minds?

Your ordinary method of correspondence with others is through discourse; anyway the Super Conscious and Unconscious Minds can't talk, your endowment of discourse is explicit to the Conscious Mind just; accordingly, you should discover another approach to speak with different personalities. The Super Conscious and Unconscious Minds don't perceive discourse; their type of correspondence is through images or pictures. This is regularly done using Tarot cards, Runes, Tea Leaves, and other "new age" techniques. While these are great approaches to impart, the vast majority of them require preparing. By and by, I will raise contemplation, for through reflection, you utilize your Conscious Mind to picture, or imagine whatever it is that you need to impart. This works very well as you may now comprehend on the grounds that you are taking what you 'find' in the outside world and disguising it using representation, as such, images and pictures.

Once you have not thought, or experience difficulty with it, here is a straightforward exercise that will assist you with learning to think and furthermore speak with your other two selves simultaneously.

Set apart some time each day for the sole reason for speaking with your Super Conscious and Unconscious Minds. Ideally, a half-hour; in any case, once that is excessively long, at that point start with 10 minutes out of each day, at that point increment to 20 minutes, and keep expanding it until you are alright with a half-hour. Once you do this all the time, you will find that it won't be long and you will be open to sitting calm for an hour or more. If you don't mind however, do your Self an enormous support and put aside in any event 10 minutes - that isn't an excessive amount to request a more joyful life, presently is it? It is significant that it is tranquil - turn off every single electronic gadget, no TV or music out of sight, no wireless, unplug the house telephone, do what you can to guarantee total calm for the designated time. Presently, take two or three full breaths and unwind. At that point tell your Unconscious Mind, in a soft tone, that you might want to become more acquainted with it better. For instance, "Hi my Unconscious Mind, I might truly want to become more acquainted with you better." Begin by requesting that it recall affectionate occasions from your youth. For instance, "It would be ideal if you help me recall some affectionate occasions from my adolescence." Then simply sit unobtrusively and see any recollections and emotions that surface.

Try not to pass judgment or break down whatever comes to you; just remember it. At the outset, your sense of self, your Conscious Mind, will probably attempt to protest you doing this - you may get the idea, This is strange, for what reason am I conversing with myself?. Just let that proceed to reaffirm to your Unconscious Mind this is essential to you and soon you find how much significant data is uninhibitedly accessible to you, in the event that you yet figure out how to tune in. Continue rehearsing this until it turns out to be natural.

At the point when it became simple for you, at that point, before you settle on any significant choices, stop and unobtrusively approach your Unconscious Mind for assistance and exhortation. When you figure out how to do this, you will understand that your Unconscious Mind will never guide you in a misguided course. It won't be long and you will have another closest companion - YOU! An expression of alert here, in some cases the Conscious (Ego) Mind will attempt to deter you from tuning in to the Unconscious Mind so to start with, don't settle on significant choices until you figure out how to know the distinction. The more you practice the reflection, the more certainty you will pick up until the distinction between your Unconscious and your Conscious-Ego psyches are completely clear.

The following thing to recall is that so as to speak with your Super Conscious Mind, you should do as such through your Unconscious Mind. We don't have an immediate association with the Super Conscious Mind and can't ordinarily discuss straightforwardly with the Super Conscious Mind; be that as it may, when you figure out how to speak with the Unconscious Mind, which thusly speaks with the Super Conscious Mind, it will in the end appear to be straightforward - as though you do have an immediate connect to your Super Conscious Mind.

To speak with our Super Conscious Mind you should send your messages through the Unconscious Mind as images or pictures and emotions. Note, if the Unconscious Mind cannot or disregards the solicitation, no message is sent to the Super Conscious Mind. That is the reason numerous supplications and perceptions don't work; the Unconscious Mind contradicts or has an issue with the solicitation. This is the reason it is so significant, even goal, to dispose of all the negative feelings that are put away in the Unconscious Mind.

A genuine case of this is assume we need an advancement or a raise at work and we approach the Super Conscious Mind for assistance to get it, however the Unconscious Mind is in fact scared of taking on the new duties that would accompany the advancement or raise because of some past injury, or negative memory. For this situation, the Unconscious Mind will just disregard, or overlook the solicitation and the Super Conscious Mind will never get the message. Consequently, when you are requesting something from the Super Conscious Mind and not getting it, ask yourself what could be blocking it in the Unconscious Mind. This is the reason it is so basic to figure out how to 'converse with' your Unconscious Mind and speak with it - so you can realize what pessimism lives there and should be wiped out.

. . .

The Super Conscious Mind, with the collaboration of the Unconscious Mind, can allow us anything we want, material or insignificant, gave the solicitation will hurt nobody.

OK, does this all bode well? Improves comprehend the maxim, "As above, so beneath?"

To outline:

We as a whole have Three Minds, a Conscious Mind, an Unconscious Mind, and a Super Conscious Mind.

The Conscious Mind is the self that we present to the world.

The Unconscious Mind remembers everything - everything that has occurred in our lives and is additionally the wellspring of our feelings or sentiments and can just impart through pictures or pictures.

The Super Conscious Mind can allow us any craving we have, however can just impart through the Unconscious Mind.

The best, albeit perhaps by all account not the only way, to speak with the Unconscious Mind is through reflection or petition.

Mind-Study In New Directions: How it Moves Healing

Mind-study, and its effect on wellbeing, has turned into an interesting endeavor as the mental age of the only remaining century unites with the data period of today. With the guide of innovation, data on mind-study has multiplied, piling up reams of information for a psyche/body association. As a matter of fact, translations of the data are diverse and inauspicious with regards to its effect on wellbeing. Disputable dubiousness encompasses mind's capacity to mend the body. Notwithstanding, the aggregate human awareness is progressing into an acknowledgment of an association among brain and prosperity. Brain and wellbeing are being reclassified to oblige the new awareness.

Mind action has been watched for a huge number of years. Generally, the subject of brain incorporates the investigation of capacities not clearly noticeable to the physical faculties, for example, care, mindfulness, astuteness, thinking, and other mental abilities. Nonetheless, innovation has enabled standard science to give proof that science and culture are synergistic. Accordingly, the subject of mind currently likewise incorporates the investigation of capacities clear to the physical faculties, for example, sensory systems, physiological responses, reflect neurons, and microtubules.

For instance, cerebrum imaging information, for example, FMRI readings, has been deciphered to check an unbreakable connection between the human personality and body, which thusly has prompted the hypothesis that psyche can be diminished to synthetic and electrical mind action. Of course, mind-mending procedures, with regards to a reducible personality, are additionally reducible, or debilitated, by the regularly changing zoo of cerebrums on the planet. Close to the way that a standard concoction and electrical cerebrum action won't be found, there is additionally the detail that reducible personality recuperating procedures are fleeting, now and then biting the dust before the mind, or the other way around.

Taking an about turn, mind-study information is additionally deciphered to publicity the longstanding hypothesis of Cartesian dualism, denoting a reasonable differentiation among brain and body, however with a mind fit for developing into more command over the body and its wellbeing. In any case, the hypothesis of a human personality as ready to control a body, or bodies, is disturbing. In addition to the fact that mind are recuperating strategies as created, or undeveloped, as the human personalities included, yet the dualistic hypothesis likewise leaves the entryway all the way open to control, lost poise.

An intriguing side-note to the dualistic hypothesis is the basic assumption that psyche is unchangeable. In all actuality, a mind separate from the body is conceivable, be that as it may, if the psyche is being decreased to a human character, it is reducible.

These investigations are not to say the present prominent personality study speculations aren't right; that isn't a point. Speculations are falsifiable and will keep on being changed as new information and disclosures rise. Human information is advancing and will conform to less prohibitive personality mending techniques as the traditional perspective of both personality and wellbeing changes with a change in perspective away from inadequate learning. Essentially, in reconsidering mind-study, and its effect on wellbeing, it is basic to comprehend the significance of conceptual translation.

For example, decreasing personality to the cerebrum, or even to quantum material science, is as unconvincing as diminishing beat to a flawless piano player. An impeccable piano player speaks to cadence, yet the piano player isn't vital for musicality's presence. In like manner, the human personality/body or even an individual (character) isn't vital for the presence of psyche. Pushing the reality further, individuals are not by any means essential for proof of mending. Careful recuperating is recognizably clear in the Mount Saint Helens locale of Washington State, which is delightfully recouping following a volcanic ejection thirty years prior.

Truly, these models likewise don't clarify brain or mind-recuperating, yet they speak to an extreme break in human awareness which thusly can build up a successful theoretical translation, even to the thought of an announcement by nineteenth century mind-healer that all is limitless Mind and its vast indication.

In spite of the fact that the presence of a vast Mind, requiring the appearance of wellbeing, runs unreasonable to the far reaching understanding that wellbeing is a condition of issue, it places a premise that can join scholars, inquires about, and laypeople the same, can drop differences, and settle the inquiry.

Is psyche and body associated? Truly, when the psyche being grouped is the human personality, its interconnectedness is with the end goal that the brain is one and equivalent to the body it encapsulates. Proof shows, that as the human personality improves, the body improves too. In any case, not generally. Since proof likewise has it that mankind is winding through an unpredictable, tangled, tangled system of transforming and fleeting associations and encounters. Hence, the inquiry is posed once more.

Is brain and body associated? No, when the psyche being perceived is the limitless Mind. The human personality/body, as we probably am aware it today, isn't even an item or appearance of vast Mind.

All in all, where does this leave the human personality/body? Precisely, where it is found, developing out of itself. The human personality/body must improve, yet not on the grounds that it in the long run develops into limitless Mind, or an appearance of perfect Mind. That won't occur. The improvement, not the human personality/body, is the truth of our reality. Extended awareness symbolizes Mind and wellbeing.

. . .

This reality, or reasonable understanding can influence the human circumstance. For example, after an awful mishap, I had severe singeing on half of my face. I didn't take advantage of confined human personality so as to fix my body. There was no mind or skin control. I didn't need torment relievers. The others conscious medical caretakers got rock out of the consumed skin as delicately as physically conceivable. My gratefulness was my experience. New skin began developing inside two days and inside three weeks, my face was totally typical, not a scar. The human personality, exemplifying harmed skin, propelled itself into non-presence, while limitless Mind and wellbeing stayed unblemished.

Mind-study, and its effect on mending, is compelling as the human personality concedes that its solitary essentialness is to perceive perfect Mind and its effect on wellbeing. Without a doubt, a Mind past the human personality is hard to see. However, at that point we don't see the way that earth is rotating around the sun at a pace of sixty-7,000 miles for every hour.

Mind-study, not the investigation of human personality, however of interminable Mind, offers a promising counter cosmology to the human focused universe. The perspective on celestial Mind, and its effect on wellbeing, foresees an encounter bereft of constrained, limited, transforming, re-wiring, crumbling, quantifiable personalities/bodies, named sound, debilitated, human, creature, or quanta. Mind-recuperating strategies never again endure the outcomes of control or dualistic clash, yet are polished based on boundless Mind and its sound sign.

Care Meditation: An approach about the Western Society

Contemplation has turned out to be incredibly prevalent in western culture in the ongoing years nonetheless; it has existed for a large number of years and has clearly finished the trial of time in different societies. Contemplation has in actuality endure 4500 years of political change and financial progress. Once reflection was not useful would regardless it be near and being drilled a huge number of years after the fact? Most likely not.

The word contemplation will in general reason perplexity in numerous individuals because of it being obscure or viewed as fairly powerful, new age, or connected with an exceptional creed or religion. Well as just talked about there is nothing surprising about reflection and I accept that the establishment for contemplation in its immaculateness isn't confounding or complex.

The very pith of reflection is straightforwardness, yet it is expressed that "effortlessness is frequently the most confounded thing. I really accept this announcement to be precise in particularly western culture's lifestyle.

Life comprises of straightforward standards, anyway individuals will in general confuse them inside their brains instead of living and being from the spirit. I know for my life, I keep reflection and living as basic as could be expected under the circumstances. I think Stephen Levine says all that needs to be said when he talked about reflection in his book, A Gradual Awakening, "contemplation is for some an outside idea, some way or another inaccessible and premonition, apparently difficult to take an interest in. Be that as it may, another word for reflection is basically mindfulness. Reflection is mindfulness. Presently, this clarification is for sure functional and down to earth to an individual needing to end up associated with contemplation.

Inside this book, I will offer a basic clarification of the procedure of contemplation, its mental, physiological, and otherworldly advantages just as a concise portrayal of my own involvement.

There are a few sorts of contemplation, anyway Levine states that "distinctions in these methods are fundamentally because of the essential book which is focused on through the procedure. Therefore, I will put together this book with respect to care reflection which includes legitimately taking an interest in every minute as it happens with however much mindfulness and understanding as could reasonably be expected. As I would like to think this is the easiest and best type of reflection and really an edified method to carry on with your day by day life. We live "now" directly at this time and that is the thing that this sort of reflection proposes. All things considered, the objective of all reflection frameworks, whatever the ideological direction or source...is to change the waking state through the products of training - to bite the dust to the life of the sense of self and be reawakened to another degree of experience.

As recently talked about, the focal point of this book will be care reflection as opposed to focus contemplation which is the thing that normally strikes a chord when the word reflection is referenced. While fixation contemplation centers around the consideration of a solitary book, mantra, or divinity, care reflection incorporates an increasingly powerful comprehensive field of perception. It is comprehensive of the profundity that encompasses us instead of closing the world out, which is progressively functional for the normal member in western culture. It was likewise recommended that care might be valuable to numerous individuals in western culture who may be reluctant to embrace Buddhist conventions or jargon. Along these lines, care reflection is significantly more suitable for our general public than talking about the full scope of contemplation procedures from eastern customs, because of its straightforwardness, common sense and saw separation from eastern ways of thinking and religions.

Instead of attempt to pick one definition to depict what care reflection is, I will introduce an assortment of perspectives from those acquainted with this particular practice so as to get the point crosswise over more briefly. As a matter of first importance, care reflection is all the more explicitly called "knowledge contemplation" in Buddhist customs, signifies "to see obviously." Mindfulness reflection is an enormous piece of Buddhism just as Zen practice; anyway it tends to be effectively rehearsed isolates from these conventions. As recently referenced it isn't important to be a rehearsing Buddhist to appreciate the products of care reflection. As of now I will present fluctuated definitions or depictions of what care reflection really is.

Albeit every one of these sections use distinctive phrasing to verbalize what care contemplation is; the general agreement comes down to "being available throughout everyday life." In my genuine belief, this likely could be the mystery that every individual have been looking for outside of themselves. Being available at the time is basic, yet significant. The vast majority will probably say, "There must be more to living than this." right?

Care contemplation centers around all zones of our being. It presents an assortment of these territories in their book, Simple Meditation and Relaxation. These components of the person incorporate being careful or mindful of your sense without judgment, monitoring your feelings with acknowledgment, keeping up familiarity with your reasoning and enabling considerations to stream by, simply taking note. Another two essential territories incorporate monitoring your breathing just as what is new with your body. What it comes down to is monitoring what is happening for you in every minute.

To further well-spoken this I will give different extracts from a care contemplation:

o Find an agreeable spot to sit, with back straight yet not unbending.

. . .

o Keep your consideration at one exact point and note the vibe that goes with every breath.

o Sounds emerge. Thought emerge. Different sensations emerge. All foundation, emerging and passing ceaselessly.

o Sensations emerge in the body, Thoughts emerge in the psyche. They go back and forth like air pockets.

o Don't get lost. Once the mind pulls away, tenderly, with a delicate non-judging, non-sticking mindfulness, come back to the breath.

o Moment to minute attention to whatever emerges, whatever exists.

My expectation is that these extracts further explain care contemplation to the peruser. Levine is an ace with regards to effortlessness in one's life just as having the ability to make reflection useful and proficient. Next, I might want to examine an assortment of intercessions utilizing care pursued by research exhibiting the mental, physiological, and otherworldly advantages. Care contemplation is really a comprehensive application and this will be appeared through the exploration discoveries talked about in this book.

MEDIATIONS

As recently talked about contemplation has been around for a great many years, anyway has as of late been incorporated into psychotherapy in western culture. The American Psychological Association, around 1977, proposed that "contemplation could encourage the restorative procedure. Lamentably, around 20 years after the fact regardless it hasn't really moved toward becoming standard. In any case, we should be blessed that some advancement is being made. Right now, I might want to talk about four current intercessions that are utilizing care contemplation as a component of the restorative procedure.

The primary intercession is the combination of care contemplation in the general psychotherapy process. An investigation talked about it as a powerful part of psychotherapy and expressed that as reflection acquires attention to emotions and inconveniences the remedial procedure, psychotherapy can give dialog and investigation of these bits of knowledge. She additionally communicates that the capacity to rehearse contemplation all through the remedial session encourages autonomy and self-authority on the customer's part. That much of the time the joining of reflection into the helpful procedure has advanced treatment and given customers a more noteworthy feeling of control and mindfulness.

In a different contextual investigation, it was depicted that coordination of care contemplation and bibliotherapy and its viability with a discouraged, upset, and jumpy customer. An investigation coordinated different readings with a transpersonal subject just as care reflection all through session. Boorstein claims that the result was noteworthy and included expanded confidence, mental and profound development and help of showing side effects. Boorstein led subsequent meet-ups and expressed that the constructive results were kept up and the customer kept on concentrating on close to home and profound development in his life.

A second well known intercession and the most regularly refered to strategy for care contemplation mediation is the program created by Jon Kabat-Zinn called Mindfulness Based Stress Reduction (MBSR). This program was grown explicitly for constant agony and stress related issue. It is a 8-multi week course for gatherings which uses a special blend of discourses identified with pressure, adapting, just as schoolwork assignments and an extraordinary guidance and routine with regards to care reflection. The capacity for customers to rehearse inside and outside of session, in actuality, circumstances is again an advantage of this methodology.

Another mediation which is emphatically connected with MBSR is Mindfulness Based Cognitive Therapy (MBCT). This mediation joins parts of psychological treatment that encourage an isolates or decentered perspective on ones contemplations including explanations, for example, Thoughts are not certainties and I am not my considerations. MBCT is intended to show abilities for recently discouraged people to watch their contemplations and emotions non-judgmentally and to consider them to be basically mental occasions that come and go as opposed to as the real world or parts of themselves.

The last mediation that I will talk about that joins care contemplation is a treatment named Dialectical Behavioral Therapy (DBT). This particular treatment was intended to treat marginal character issue anyway it is at present being applied to a wide range of populaces. DBT incorporates care contemplation preparing with subjective social aptitudes so as to encourage acknowledgment and change simultaneously. Explicit parts of this mediation incorporate passionate guideline, relational abilities, and pain resistance aptitudes. In my own vocation I have had direct involvement with this a dependence office and saw it as very powerful. Private customers grasped the care segments in all parts of their lives and appeared to really profit by rehearsing acknowledgment and non-judgment as a feature of their recuperation. I really trust that more mediations will end up accessible and care reflection will in the end get the regard it merits in the field of psychotherapy and life by and large.

Care contemplation is an all-encompassing device for development and mindfulness. It benefits the brain, body, and soul all in all, anyway for this books reason I will isolate the parts into the advantages identified with mental, philosophical, and otherworldly components of the person. These will be founded on the writing relating to care reflection explicitly and what has been talked about in an assortment of research contemplates.

PHYSIOLOGICAL BENEFITS

The writing talks about a colossal measure of physiological advantages got from care reflection. To list and talk about every one of them is past the extent of this book; anyway I will examine a portion of the fundamental physical advantages appeared all through the experimental writing. Initially, the physiological changes that have been seen when rehearsing contemplation, for example, diminished pulse, breathing and the bringing down of circulatory strain has been named the "unwinding reaction". These progressions can obviously be amazingly advantageous to those people expecting to get away from the everyday stress and mayhem of society. Be that as it may, the physiological advantages of care reflection rise above the transitory changes during the demonstration of contemplation.

In an investigation, he examined a huge range of advantages that were found in his scrutiny of the accessible research. These included increment cardiovascular yield, muscle unwinding, expanded serotonin and melatonin levels, and huge improvement in ceaseless torment. Also care contemplation was seen as advantageous for psoriases, epilepsy, fibromyalgia, and hypertension. This concise rundown clearly shows that care contemplation can be powerful for the body part of an individual. We should investigate the other two components that make up individuals.

MENTAL

Various mental advantages of care reflection are referenced all through the exact writing. Once more, this isn't a comprehensive survey of the writing, however a short explanation of results detailed with respect to the act of care reflection. It further clarifies the advantages of care reflection as far as its passionate advantages concerning self-development. In her book she clarifies that mind-boggling sentiments are better ready to be acknowledged as an individual can possess these emotions and experience them with a more prominent feeling of security.

Some experimental examinations that can be surveyed:

o Increased satisfaction

o Increased satisfaction

o Increased positive musings

o Increase critical thinking aptitudes

o Enhanced acknowledgment

o Enhanced empathy

o Enhanced resilience

o Increased unwinding

o Increased strength

. . .

o Better control of sentiments and moral duty

o Improvement in mental prosperity

o Decreased nervousness

o Decreased substance misuse

It talked about care contemplation's capacity to enable patients to comprehend that there are no fast arrangements in life which prompts advancement of tolerance in their self-improvement venture. Furthermore, the advancement of a non-judgmental frame of mind just as the capacity to deal with what is instead of what could have been.

The result of some of these examinations included diminished self-reports of by and large mental trouble, including sorrow, decreased self-reports of state and attribute uneasiness and expanded scores of sympathy levels. Once more, in the mental space clearly care reflection has huge advantages.

PROFOUND

Profound advantages are additionally exhibited in the training and utilization of care contemplation. In a study, it was additionally discovered that there were expanded scores on the proportions of profound encounters, which fundamentally implied that following the care presentation, members had a more noteworthy conviction of the presence of a higher power just as an expansion in the disguise of an individual cozy relationship to a higher power. It was noticed that care reflection helps a patient or individual to confide in their internal nature and intelligence. At last, contemplation is "accessible as an apparatus for the individuals who wish to plumb the profundities of their own being and investigate the idea of brain, character, and cognizance. It's an apparatus that can be utilized from the earliest starting point as far as possible of the otherworldly mission". Clearly, there are numerous other profound advantages of contemplation, including the self-evident, Nirvana; anyway I simply provided the peruser with an outline. Maybe, it might rouse some to enter this adventure of mindfulness and investigate the numerous extra diamonds along the way.

INDIVIDUAL EXPERIENCE

The point of life is to live, and to live intends to be alert, blissfully, unsteadily, calmly, supernaturally mindful." This is the thing that care contemplation has brought to my life. Definitely, don't imagine that I sit in reflection ceaselessly and segregate from the world. Care enables me to feel each snapshot of life inside my whole existence. It enables me to live as opposed to simply existing and the use of this training all through the previous five years of my life has changed who I am. I have taken advantage of my authentic being and joined with the vitality of the universe. Basically by developing familiarity with the minute through care I have had the option to rise above my sense of self and travel every day on the way of self-completion. I have encountered the unadulterated quintessence of care contemplation. Every snapshot of my life permits constant practice and use of this fundamental ability that truly gives life. Every individual on this planet has the intrinsic capacity to take advantage of the flawlessness and accuracy of care contemplation. Proceed to encounter the happiness that it offers.

At last, all through this book I have examined what care contemplation is, gave an assortment of depiction by the specialists in this training, and given the peruser instances of the procedure of care reflection dependent on works by Stephen Levine. It was finished up, that just care contemplation is monitoring life, which clearly can be rehearsed in any setting. Care intercession is very pragmatic in the west and has been used in an assortment of restorative mediations with much achievement. Also, it has been appeared to have physiological, mental, and otherworldly advantages by the exploration so far. To put it plainly, care intervention is an incredible device for the entire individual to use toward individual and otherworldly development. Care is really living in this exact instant. Go really live in the now and experience the genuine quintessence of existence without the hoodwinked obstructions caused the reasoning personality.

Are Mindfulness and Meditation Evil concepts?

Nowadays, talks of reflection and care show up wherever from business and medicinal diaries, to fixation and injury recuperation gatherings, to instruction meetings. In this book, you'll realize why such huge numbers of are going to these strategies and how to stay away from normal confusions, perils, and potential traps.

By ongoing reports, you may think contemplation and care are a "panacea" (fix just for) everything that upsets you. Projects are growing up in clinics for agony the board, in detainment facilities for prisoner change, and in military, police, and crisis reaction settings to help handle exceptional circumstances and recoup from PTSD.

These systems are utilized as a help in psychotherapy-for habit and injury recuperation, defusing self-harm, expanding mindfulness, and subduing self-analysis. They are progressively looked for after for managing the pressure of living in our quick paced, risk touchy world. To sustain this interest, innumerable applications guarantee to offer the advantages of these practices at the push of a catch.

However, with the ascent in prominence of care and contemplation, I've started to see some contrarian features, for example, "New Study Shows Meditation Doesn't Make You Happier, More Creative,"

"Reflection Not a Panacea," or "Christians Should Be Wary of Meditation."

As a reflection instructor, I hear starting understudies make statements like:

• "Reflection should unwind however it made me aggravated."

• "Reflection should feel better, yet it made me progressively worried."

• "I figured contemplation would enable me to rest, yet it gave me bad dreams."

• "I thought contemplation should enable me to acknowledge myself, yet it made me increasingly self-basic."

• "I am more mindful of my lack of caution than any other time in recent memory. How is this helping me?"

(Indication: Meditation doesn't "cause these things to occur." It uncovers them. Contemplation and care make you progressively mindful of what's going on in your intuitive personality.)

How about we demystify reflection and care by characterizing them unmistakably, so you can survey their capacity and viability, get misinterpretations, and keep away from threats and potential entanglements.

Reflection and Mindfulness Defined

By reflection I signify, "Carefully concentrating on a particular central item for a while." It's tied in with preparing your psyche to intentionally concentrate. It's that direct.

A central book in reflection can be the vibes of breathing, a mantra or centering phrase, the flood of your contemplations and sentiments, the nearness of God, a clear divider, or a light fire. Concentrating on picked central books builds up your capacity to focus, be available, and completely connect with what you are doing.

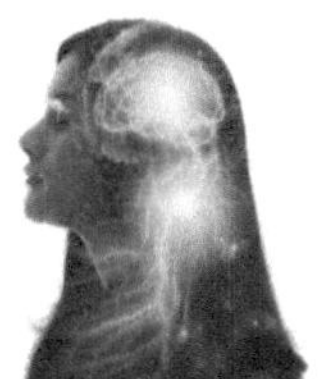

"Carefully" in the definition implies that you work out "care" during contemplation. Care signifies, "focusing, intentionally, right now, without judgment." at the end of the day, you embrace the mentality of an inquisitive eyewitness, simply seeing what's going on without passing judgment on it as "fortunate or unfortunate." A non-judgmental demeanor empowers you to see all the more obviously, rather than responding from dread, inclination, or partiality which contort understanding.

To summarize, "contemplation" is a consideration preparing system and "care" is a successful demeanor for rehearsing this procedure. You could likewise say that reflection is a chance to rehearse care. Together, reflection and care give you a more profound comprehension of how your mind functions.

Here's the way it goes by and by:

As you think about a particular central book, you see minutes when your mind strays to different things, for example, a contention you had yesterday, a cherished memory, an introduction you have later today, or what you may have for lunch. Care empowers you to perceive when and where your mind meanders, acknowledge this as something a bustling personality does, and tenderly return your regard for your picked central item.

During contemplation, you will have an entire host of various musings and emotions. Some may feel better: some may alarm you. Care regards them no different as passing bits of data. Utilizing care, you come to understand that all musings and sentiments go back and forth. They offer data, yet they are not any more significant than that. They are not something to fear when you approach them carefully. This knowledge can liberate you from uneasiness about what is happening inside you.

MEDITATION: THE CONCEPT OF THE 3RS

I consider the way toward dealing with your brain during reflection the 3Rs: Recognize, Release, and Return. You perceive when you have meandered from your place of center, discharge focusing on that "interruption," and come back to your picked object of consideration. It's that straightforward.

In any case, similar to any educated ability, it very well may challenge from the start. You may discover your mind meanders more often than not. You may end up got up to speed in negative considerations and sentiments. You may end up disturbed, self-basic, exhausted, or thinking about whether you're doing it right-or in case you're doing anything by any means!

That is OK. Perceiving the majority of this is a piece of reflection. Reflection expands mindfulness. You do this by carefully concentrating, perceiving and tolerating what your brain does, discharging interruptions, and coming back to your picked center over and over and once more.

As you rehash this procedure, you build up a feeling of simplicity with dealing with your musings and sentiments and an opportunity to pick what you center around and what you discharge. By rehearsing care during contemplation, you develop your capacity to identify with a wide range of minutes in your existence without breaking a sweat.

FURTHER BENEFITS OF PRACTICE

As you ponder for a while (state 10-20 minutes) reliably, your mind calms down, your feelings quiet, and your body unwinds. You de-pressurize, let go of over-thinking, and discharge developed pressure. As you discharge pressure, vitality is opened up that your body and mind use to recuperate, fix, coordinate, and mend.

You begin to feel like yourself once more. You understand that "what your identity is" is significantly more than "the prattle" in your brain or the feelings that can "take you over." You are a more profound seeing nearness who "has" musings, sentiments, and encounters, however isn't characterized by them. This can be a life changing revelation!

These advantages don't occur on the grounds that you are attempting to clear your psyche, they occur because of rehearsing the 3Rs. As you practice reliably, you build up the abilities of perceiving where your psyche is engaged, discharging what isn't serving you or others, and coming back to what is important most.

These are priceless abilities that serve you in anything you need to do, survive, or achieve. I would venture to such an extreme as to state they are crucial aptitudes you have to carry on with your life well. Why, at that point, would you say you weren't encouraged these fundamental abilities in school when you were youthful? Notwithstanding the reasons, at any age, you can learn them with a couple of basic guidelines, understanding into how they work, and steady practice.

Actually, I like to rehearse before anything else. For quite a bit of my life, I woke up inclination on edge about what I needed to do in the day ahead. However, presently, regardless of how I feel when I wake up, I feel loose and focused after my morning practice. I have a quiet reference point I can come back to when I get aggravated or worried, made up for lost time in antagonism, or feel overpowered by what's going on in my general surroundings.

WHY MINDFULNESS AND MEDITATION: IMPORTANCE

Today there are interminable requests on our time, vitality, and consideration and they call to us all day, every day making us feel as though we generally should accomplish something profitable. We feel constrained to react in a split second via web-based networking media and accumulate a constant flow of tempting bits of data to keep us educated and interested. Indeed, even amusement turns into an "absolute necessity do" as we feel constrained to marathon watch to get "made up for lost time" with however much pleasure as could be expected in our "spare time."

HOWEVER CONTINUALLY BEING "IN A HURRY" ISN'T SOUND.

Our bodies and minds are not made to keep running in consistent overdrive. We are intended to participate in movement, at that point to rest and recuperate from what we've done. In our vacation, our body fixes itself, coordinates all that we've encountered, and recuperates cell harm we've continued.

. . .

Once we don't respect this equalization, our frameworks go haywire. We get depleted, hold expanding levels of pressure in our bodies, and become industriously restless or discouraged. In this "overcooked" state, we welcome the host of incessant ailments like malignant growth, coronary illness, and auto-invulnerable issue that are scourge.

Contemplation is an organized break from this action, so you can concentrate internally, rest, and recoup. From the start, it might want to do "nothing," be that as it may, as we've seen, the procedure is a delicate, yet dynamic, preparing of your brain. It enables you to step over from the frenzied pace of life, deliberately loosen up, and see what's happening inside.

Reflection and care uncover your internal operations. They reveal the intuitive predispositions that lead to contentions, misguided thinking, and terrible choices. They sparkle a light on propensities that drive undesirable outcomes throughout your life. They help you all the more impartially see what you are doing, so you can intentionally pick solid propensities and let go of unfortunate ones.

Possibly in particular for us in this hyper-driven buyer culture, they urge us to back off, take a full breath, and focus on the connections, blessings, and openings we as of now have, as opposed to continually attempting to be, have, and accomplish more.

MEDITATION AND MINDFULNESS DANGEROUS: THE END APPROACH

Are reflection and care risky? Indeed. They take steps to make you progressively cognizant and deliberate. They are risky to your negative musings, emotions, practices, and convictions. They discharge the smothering grasp of dread, predisposition, and bias. They sparkle a light on what requirements to change.

By rehearsing care in contemplation, you figure out how to assess all sides of any circumstance all the more unbiasedly, so you can settle on better choices. You perceive what never again serves you and others, so you can move your time, vitality, and regard for what does. What's more, you become progressively present, centered, and completely occupied with your encounters, so you carry on with a more extravagant, increasingly deliberate life.

YOUR MIND IS YOUR GREATEST POWER

Thus, we should attempt to clarify why your brain is your most prominent power. Everything in our universe, just as such seems stable in our physical world, is comprised of vibrations of vitality. Indeed, even our considerations are made by these vibrating waves, and are the most unique and liquid substance in the whole universe.

Is it accurate to say that you are directing your heart to thump at the present time? Assuming no, what does? How can it impact you?

To start with, your contemplations are autonomous of the physical universe, but then it communicates with it. Is astounding that any idea that is rehashed again and again in your cognizant personality will at that point make an engraving into your subliminal.

Furthermore, when this imprint makes it into your oblivious personality, it is then utilized as a tuning device and starts vibrating, and draws in to you the individuals, the conditions, and the occasions that match the pictures that you have inside. You have a genuine capacity to impact and direct the things that transpire.

INFLUENCE: THE POWER TO SUBDUE

In this way, let me make a point before you consider me in dismay. It is hard for you to think about that you can accomplish certain things, or are adequate, or effective or rich. However you accept the inverse to be valid. Hence, for what reason would it be unimaginable for your brain to trust one way yet not the other?

A lovely aspect regarding the subliminal and its capacity is that it can't differentiate between what is genuine and what you envision. So it implies that you can program and engraving into it anything you need.

Thus, tests have been done about this where competitors fundamentally envision rehearsing for a month and after that do just as the individuals who did to be sure practice. It brought about their mind accepting that they were great which improved their presentation. Hence, envisioning an activity or a condition of being in your brain again and again makes a significant engraving on your subliminal.

THE POWERFUL SOURCE WITHIN

The Soviet Union utilized it on their competitors, I know, I was one of them. Be that as it may, what is significantly more prominent is that it goes past game and can be utilized for accounts, connections, vocation, and self-mending. There are no parts of your life unthinkable when you work with mind control techniques. It tends to be representation, pondering, certifications, fascination or making new convictions. You have a feeling that you assume responsibility for your life.

Your considerations are the most staggeringly amazing wellspring of sustenance and wealth. In any case, no one shows us how to think. We figure out how to be certain or do as well as can be expected. All things considered, I am heartbroken, yet that is tragic. Positive reasoning is principal while mind power is an incredible asset available to you.

Furthermore, the laws and techniques can be promptly comprehended by anybody. It is a genuine arousing once you understand that your musings impact your world. Once you do have confidence at the top of the priority list control, you are in front of a huge number of different people, since despite everything it is basically an ongoing hypothesis. Just a little level of the world puts stock in it, and half of those don't rehearse it every day or in the correct manner.

MIND POWER; DEFINITION

Mind power isn't simply being sure; it is utilizing approaches to engrave convictions and pictures, not just on a cognizant level all things considered with positive intuition however on an oblivious level. When you envision and live the stuff you need, over and over, you are pulling in those things to you.

Furthermore, there is no more prominent defining moment in your life than to find that you have an individual power, and that you are the ace of your predetermination. And everything necessary is possibly fifteen minutes per day to change your life once you are prepared to rehearse day by day.

In any case, recall that it can work similarly against you. The explanation being is that your considerations can likewise keep you in neediness, in ailment, or not prevail at your objectives. Indeed, it is probably the best disaster of today. It is the reason the vast majority are not excelling. Their mind control intuitively pulls in an inappropriate things in their lives. In truth, your contemplations are what is making your world.

MIND POWER AND CREATIVITY

Imaginative individuals frequently produced developments through thoughts appearing unexpectedly, however consistently when they took a break. These things don't occur when you are excessively occupied or buckling down. You should give yourself great quality time and respect yourself. So you have to take opportunity days where you don't work by any stretch of the imagination.

What's more, when you let go of everything, you give a period your inventiveness and instinct to connect with the wealth of contemplations and mind influence you have at your mien.

For what reason do I generally get my best thoughts in the shower?

In this way, even a little league away can have any kind of effect. Today, I am a major devotee to simply getting some much needed rest sometimes to reflect, survey and assess things. In the event that you pull in the things that are at a similar recurrence you are the point at which you are pushed or exhausted, it won't benefit you in any way.

ACCOMPLISH SOMETHING YOU LOVE

You are a splendid human machine with mind control! What I have acknowledged is that every single fruitful individuals I know made their fortune and met accomplishment in a zone that they cherished. Think for a second! Has anybody at any point made a lot of cash by accomplishing something that they abhor?

I without a doubt don't! Steve Jobs got into PCs since he adored it and needed to have any kind of effect, not on the grounds that he needed to be rich. That is one of the privileged insights of achievement also. So discover something that you want to do. In addition to the fact that you will be progressively fruitful at it you will have a ton of fun doing it.

62

Along these lines, you win the two different ways. However, one of the adages of mind power is that you should comprehend what you need before you can get it. Furthermore, you need to ensure that your objectives are joined to a strategic, or reason, or it won't last.

MIND POWER: THE FIRST STEP

The excellent thing about existence is that we get the chance to pick whatever objectives we need. It is magnificent! When there is unrestrained choice, everyone has the option to live their reality distinctively and have their meaning of achievement.

As time passes by, and you look at your objectives now and again, you may discover that your inspirations are not as precise as you at first suspected they would be. Along these lines, you would prefer not to wind up ascending the stepping stool of accomplishment, just to find that it is facing an inappropriate divider. What's more, that is the reason every one of us, in due time, have an emotional meltdown.

Thus, the initial step to mind control and to changing your life is to focus on the contemplations inside your brain. And after that immediate them as needs be. Consistently, you have a large number of considerations. So when you understand that they impact, influence and help to make your existence, you should turn out to be exceptionally aware of what you are thinking.

WRONG BELIEFS: THE IMPRINTS

It works with any part of your life however how about we take the case of cash. What do you for the most part feel when you think about it? Is it that cash is hard to make? Do you accept that there are nothing more than a bad memory open doors out there? Or then again is it that you appear to be never to have enough cash?

What's more, once these are the sort of contemplations you think, at that point shockingly what's going on is you are engraving that reality into your subliminal. Just by your everyday stressing and worry over cash, you engrave your oblivious with a shortage cognizance. So once something is imprinted in your intuitive personality, it at that point starts to draw in the individuals, conditions, and occasions that match the pictures that you have inside.

So you are blocking yourself in an endless encounter of disappointment on attempting to excel monetarily. Furthermore, it doesn't make a difference how long a day you work or the thoughts you have. In the event that your convictions about cash are constraining, at that point you won't show cash.

THE KEY ASPECT OF MIND POWER

Presently, the inverse is similarly substantial. It is the lovely thing about mind control. Reiteration is one of the key parts of getting things. Your intuitive will acknowledge any idea or conviction that you ceaselessly engrave. Furthermore, fortunately you can reinvent and engrave new thriving convictions.

So you should simply to rehash things again and again, and trust it to be valid. What's more, what will happen is that step by step it will take an engraving, and it will change your convictions about cash. What's more, as you turn your perspectives around; your mind power starts to draw in better circumstances to you.

In this manner, you have to focus on the progression of considerations inside your brain. Investigate those which are reliable with what you want. Once you don't have the correct contemplations, at that point you have to divert your brain to another spot of convictions through mind control procedures. Furthermore, build up another flourishing awareness.

THE SECOND STEP TO MIND POWER

The main success conviction is that it is an inexhaustible universe. You need to perceive thriving all over and to fill your psyche with inclination, seeing, detecting and being encompassed by riches. Get an espresso at the most costly spot you know and invest energy there. Or on the other hand take a gander at your preferred vehicle and sit in it, envisioning you possess it.

Truth be told, your mind power couldn't care less about your sex, your otherworldly confidence, or the shade of your skin. There are numerous individuals getting to be moguls in this world. They are not in the slightest degree unique in relation to you. With flourishing convictions, smart thoughts, activity and discovering your calling, there are no reasons why you will fail.

Along these lines, you simply need to discover something that you like. Regardless of whether you pick just to do what you adore, despite everything you have countless chances to work and be fruitful. Another conviction is that it is your obligation and duty to prevail as 'Uncle G' consistently says.

RESPECT YOUR MIND'S INSTINCT

Subsequently, you need to respect what is calling you since that isn't just what is going to make you fruitful yet in addition is your commitment to the world. You need to tune in to that little call that guides you to proceed onward. I don't state it will be simple or that you won't get a couple of restless evenings over it until you settle on the choice.

Be that as it may, once you respect your mind control impulse, it may the best choice you can ever make. In the event that you pursue what you adore, you may contact more individuals' lives. Thus, you need to pursue your rapture, or what makes you bounce for delight.

You can bring home the bacon accomplishing something you don't care for, yet you will never be enormously effective.

Yet, the most intriguing, testing and energizing is that by picking your musings, you can direct and impact your activities. What's more, you can make the vibrations of vitality you need inside you that will draw in substances to you.

THE UNLIMITED MIND POWER AT YOUR DISPOSAL

Mind power is extremely strong. You should understand that you have boundless power available to you. So go through five to ten minutes daily examining, thinking and insisting the contemplations you need to yourself. A few days, you may be energized after this little exercise. In any case, there will different occasions where that little voice comes in and says "Who are you joking? You don't have boundless power."

Be that as it may, the basic factor here is to do it consistently. Never miss a day, regardless of whether it is energizing or irritating to do. Mind power needs reiteration. What's more, some place along the ninety-day time frame, as engraving requires significant investment, you will feel like an enabling conviction is assuming control over you. At some point, it may take longer.

In this way, it is the thing that has the effect between positive reasoning and mind control. The previous is about "Think positive and positive things will transpire." There is nothing incorrectly about that; I preferably you imagine that path over adversely. In any case, personality power is making it a stride past that.

MIND POWER AND SUCCESS

Mind power causes you to characterize unmistakably what it is you need. At that point through specific strategies, for example, confirmations, perception, engraving, making new convictions, you include them through reiteration. So the intuitive personality starts to get on it.

In this way, give yourself the correct messages and do some deal with it every day as it doesn't occur mystically. Make a rundown of fifteen to twenty things that make you feel better and fruitful about who and what you are currently. What's more, the key here is 'Now.'

However, you frequently consider the objectives you need to accomplish. Things that you will do, or be or the progressions you are going to make. It is okay to take a gander at the future, and yet, you need to make a vibration of achievement now. Keep in mind: achievement draws in more achievement.

MAKE YOUR MIND POWER NOW

In this manner, record and make a rundown of things that make you have an inclination that you have achievement now. At that point go through five minutes every day going over it and as you read it, feel effective about who and what you are NOW. It very well may be straightforward things like "I am an incredible cook," I am a decent companion," "I dress well," "I am savvy," and that's just the beginning.

Therefore, it will start making a triumph vibration now, with the goal that this recurrence pulls in to it other future victories. It is an entirely basic but then convincing strategy. At the point when you start your day thusly, you start it with a triumph vibration.

What's more, concerning representation, it is engraving into your psyche the accurate objective, seeing, feeling, tasting, and vibrating what you need to transpire. However, one of the stunts with envisioning is that you have to take a gander at it as it is now happening now and not later on.

So here you have it! Mind power is an integral asset that every one of us has. Be that as it may, you need to change your point of view on life, and be thankful. Along these lines currently, make the most of your new capacity by utilizing it completely in light of the fact that, in all honesty, you have boundless power available to you.

THE MIND: THE SCIENCE OF NOT BECOMING

Here is another science. Nay, it isn't new. Master Shreekrishna in the epic Mahabharatha knew it. He named it as separation/dispassion. In any case, he couldn't engender a compelling strategy for accomplishing it. Along these lines, till today it stayed as a philosophical statute never setting out to enter the boondocks of science.

Presently a spiritualist named Sadguru Jaggi Vasudev hailing from southern districts of India spreads the craft of not turning into the psyche. As indicated by him re-designing the inward world is the one of a kind answer for heap issues rising on the planet outside. What's more, "separating from the brain" is the instrument for it.

In this time of innovation upheaval, bolstered by logical confirmations he technologizes the approaches to tame the human personalities of the 21st century. He cut off his procedures from any notion of religion and tended to it as designing inward building. He initiated it as skeptical, logical system. So as to avoid potential hindrances that deny access to these strategies, he made this striking stride. In his blog, he reports logical confirmations for the incalculable advantages of his procedure by expressing the consequences of studies which is particularly dependable to the extent ordinary factually arranged research practices are concerned. Visit the Isha Yoga blog for confirmations

Padmasree Jaggi Vasudev, says there are just musings... nothing worth mentioning or awful contemplations... just considerations. As indicated by him, similarly as the heart thumps, kidney and liver capacities mind will continue popping considerations from its store of information. Similarly as one can not prevent the liver from working or change the substance of its working at a specific time, one can't stop or redirect mind (for long) as one wish during waking hours. However, one can coexist with challenges emerging from this endless reusing of musings by making an agreeable good ways from it.

So a science is advancing. The study of not turning into the brain. It isn't by disregarding the psyche. Nor by smothering the psyche. Nor by occupying consideration from the brain. Be that as it may, by making a "separation" among you and your brain. Building up that capacity is the essence of strategies upheld by internal designing. Has present day brain research at any point thought of this plausibility of making the separation?.

CARE ISN'T SUFFICIENT

Care is an idea that bears a tint of this system. In any case, it never goes past getting to be mindful of musings, feelings, and thought processes of one's psyche. Getting to be mindful of one's psychological exchanges and thought processes behind it encourage a superior hold over one's mental state. This is the presumption behind care. In any case, that isn't adequate.

Getting to be mindful of complexities of one's psyche doesn't liberate one from the impact of those complexities. It might help in progressing down the complexities somewhat. In any case, for reasons unknown or other when the mindfulness loosens the mind will assume control over the individual and restore its grip over him. The individual will again fall into the groove of being constrained by his very own psyche.

There is an enormous distinction between not relating to your musings and not relating to your psyche. In the main case, we must be specific. Also, it is our tact which figures out which musings are to be kept detached while relating to progressively sound ones. In the second, one spotlights on structure up a specific degree of poise regardless of the sort and substance of contemplations. In this sense, making a good ways from (not relating to) the psyche is an all-encompassing methodology.

The craft of turning into an aloof passerby is not the same as making a good ways from the brain. Turning into one's very own passerby psyche is a demonstration which requires an enormous measure of vitality as various musings are accused of various degrees of enthusiastic vitality. Keeping the mind enduring for quite a while even in the uneven deluge of considerations is almost unthinkable by acting oneself like an inactive passerby. Since, concentrating on keeping up a specific degree of latency drains vitality assets as the drive to react/respond is held under control. When this central vitality runs out the influxes of considerations ricochet back and vanquishes the mindfulness.

KEEPING GOOD WAYS FROM THE PSYCHE

As we grow up we keep a good ways from what we feel as stunning or wrong. At the point when mind builds up the youngster tosses teddy bear into the dustbin and connects with progressively reasonable things which suit its perceptual resources. We lose enthusiasm for things which doesn't fit into our feeling of the real world and keep a good ways from them or surrender them inside and out. So for what reason would it be a good idea for one to keep a good ways from brain? Is it on the grounds that the psyche is defective or incredible? The appropriate response is a decided YES. The brain can never be flawless and it isn't genuine either.

The demonstration of making a sound good ways from brain gets its legitimacy from the perceptual confinement with which individuals are conceived. Our view of anything under the sky is fractional. Logical confirmations envoy the deficiency of perceptual resources of human faculties and contemplations got from them.

For instance, if our eyes were impeccable there would not have been magnifying lens in the labs. So musings include a supply of information we gathered and put away with the assistance of our blemished discerning abilities. They are dead and invalid when we gauge every one of them against supreme reality. Great just as awful musings that we isolate by alluding to our ethical models are simply contemplations accused of deficiencies of shifting degrees. They are inalienable with perceptual blunders. All considerations are similarly flawed. An idea we consider as cooperative attitude be outrightly more awful in some other culture. Goodness and disagreeableness haven't any all-inclusive legitimacy. Be that as it may, the condition of perceptual deficiency with which each thinking is shaded has all inclusive legitimacy.

An individual who is persuaded of this genuine nature of the considerations which structure the very texture of his mind will never credit an excess of significance to them. Or maybe it will furnish him with important preparation to make a good ways from them. It's anything but difficult to keep a good ways from a thing that isn't probably going to serve our expectations of prosperity and joy.

INFORMATION ABOUT THE CONSTRAINTS OF THE HUMAN PERSONALITY MUST BE SPREAD

For the study of "not turning into the brain" to advance, a specific reorientation in the manner in which brain research depicts the human personality is required. Acknowledgment of constraints of manner of thinking and resulting idea development ought to be the inspiration to keep a good ways from the psyche. The characteristic insufficiency, defect, and deficiency in human discernment and resulting applied arrangement must be acknowledged and proliferated. Not in the feeling of disparaging the tremendous capability of the human personality. In any case, information about the deficiency and confinements which exist together with the intellectual capacities must get dissemination in a similar range as the conceivable outcomes and possibilities of the human personality.

Imperfectness in recognition and ends framed about day by day life occasions is a reality with which creation has presented to with human intellectual capacities. Formulating viable approaches to persuade human personalities of this reality must be one of the cardinal destinations of every single mental hypothesis and research attempts.

Customary brain science needs to perceive any individual or social variations in conduct, propensities, convictions recognitions, perceptions and so forth as psychological wellness issues. It has numerous treatments, systems in its toolbox custom-made to roll out great prompt improvements in the people with issues. Shouldn't something be said about taking a gander at these distortions as very normal and as coming about because of widespread imperfectness or deficiencies of human intellectual capacities? Shouldn't something be said about changing the criteria for evaluating basic mental issue (CMD)?. Shouldn't something be said about engendering the craft of "not turning into one's very own brain" or keeping a good ways from one's own psyche as a cure to every mental issue that come in the method for human mental prosperity?

LAST WORD

A tremendous volume of human potential lay stuck and stays dead in light of the fact that a lion's share of people are captives to their manner of thinking or mental complexities. Efficiency in numerous domains of human working endures in light of the fact that people are occupied with fixing their contemplations trusting that they can stay them in some protected spot and stroll back to composure and happiness sometime in the not so distant future. Be that as it may, they get snared in the perpetual unrest of point of view. They put some distance between numerous conceivable outcomes and measurements for development.

Contemplations are not constantly uneven and difficult to oversee however they are not constantly requested and quiet either. Staying consistent in the unending vacillation can be conceivable just when we make an agreeable good ways from the brain. Give the cutting edge brain research a chance to spread a culture of "mental development" which can be achieved by removing from the psyche. The record of the prosperity of the human populace will rise ever time high by this.

It appears there is a panacea for every single mental unsettling influence humankind of twenty first century faces. Another science is developing. This science rises above the customary mental methodologies like care, metacognition and so forth. It has something new to say the humankind regarding his defective personality. This science gets its legitimacy from the all-inclusive imperfectness with which human personality is made. It states the requirement for separating from the brain all together not to be constrained by the psyche. To end subjection to one's very own psyche, ace that craft of not getting to be mind.

PEACE OF MIND AND GET OVER DEPRESSION AND ANXIETY : THE MOST EFFECTIVE METHOD TO ENJOY

Without a doubt, the individual on the opposite side of the entryway is furious and needs to some have genuine feelings of serenity and calm. This sort of approach to discover significant serenity is shallow, one that is stunning and self-evident.

There's another method to have genuine feelings of serenity most of individuals try for. It's a quiet cognizant personality.

Being irate and upset and unfit to have genuine feelings of serenity will keep you conscious after a long time after night.

The more drawn out this continues, the more complete the harms will wind up being.

It can prompt looking through how to get over despondency and other tension related issues.

The majority of this negative reasoning dirties the psyche unnecessarily. Void your brain of all these horrible propensities and start to have true serenity in day by day life.

Try not to leave your mind empty for long to stay away from it from reclining to the horrible side.

The Course in Miracles states, "Hear not its franticness, and accept not the outlandish is valid."

Continue relinquishing every single ominous idea by discharging them from your brain, and have significant serenity with ideal and rousing thoughts.

By rehashing this strategy, you are rehearsing superb propensities planned for keeping your mind without troublesome contemplations and loaded with positive vibrations to have and achieve true serenity.

Take a stab at envisioning serene scenes in your brain. You can at first imagine in your mind a sea shore being battered by tropical stormy climate conditions.

Everything is by all accounts scattered, like a troubled personality.

A pained personality takes after a tempest in your psyche. Mean to develop a solid structure of uplifting frames of mind with the goal that when another tempest hits your psyche, you're set up to face it.

This is the manner by which your perspective ought to be, serene with the goal that it very well may be utilized to have genuine feelings of serenity in day by day life.

You can in like manner join gathering talks where the dialog is focused on the most proficient method to discover true serenity in concordance with adoration, harmony, and euphoria. At the point when you state, "I Want Peace of Mind."

Once you want to be without anyone else, snapshots of quietness can enable you to have genuine feelings of serenity.

Get books on discovering genuine feelings of serenity that suggest solace and you may be able to find different intends to secure your target.

By rehashing this procedure, you are rehearsing the propensities for fruitful individuals, and keeping your mind absolutely free of negative thoughts and brimming with positive vibrations to accomplish genuine feelings of serenity.

Keep in mind a battling psyche resembles a tempest in your brain.

To genuine feelings of serenity in everyday life!

Where it counts in a perpetual field of your mind rest your mind control insider facts, in the oblivious personality which houses your fanciful sense of self. This sense of self isn't genuine, however it thinks it is and trusts it is associated with your recognizable proof.

The sense of self has anticipated as a body, called human.

As such, your self image character is a piece of your entire personality that activities and dreams pictures of what it believes is this present reality, and accepts is you.

Each part analyzes inevitably so as to make your character. Around there that fantasies of fantasy, you are torpid, uninformed, however you have computerized activities that occur.

Continue perusing to comprehend the propensities for fruitful individuals who have ever strolled this world have scholarly personality control privileged insights, by how to be responsible for the sense of self instead of the inner self controlling them

Once in a while, you are unconscious since the oblivious personality disguises numerous components that trigger such cataleptics.

A case of the oblivious personality's exercises anyway is remembered by the projections which are regularly suppositions.

This is the reason the Course in Miracles states, "You, my kid, fear your siblings and of your Father and of yourself. You are just deluded in them."

What happened is your oblivious personality sent a sign that diverted to the subliminal personality. The two of these fellers got together for a minute and evoked an apathetic thought into your psyche.

How would I comprehend when the oblivious personality is connecting?

You build up mindfulness of mind control privileged insights with a proceeding with more noteworthy feeling of mindfulness.

We have programmed responses originating from the oblivious personality, which instinctually triggers automatic movement, considerations and activities. Reflex reaction causes us accidentally to respond to these sign.

How would I deal with these programmed activities?

You don't basically control these activities, except if the sign are sending negative messages. Because of the way that we are influenced by bearings and effects, to find these mind control privileged insights we have to figure out how to recognize why we feel explicit ways or accomplish certain things.

Should remain conscious consistently to reveal mind control privileged insights?

Actually no, not in any manner, some portion of understanding these mind control privileged insights is by understanding why your body, or, self image, needs its rest.

Perhaps the best strategy to familiarize you with mind control privileged insights is to utilize self-converse with let go of such inner self jokes.

The Course in Miracles instructs us to, "Solicit what they are from the Teacher of Reality, and hearing His answer, you also will chuckle at your feelings of dread and supplant them with harmony."

Once we recognize this conscience character, it helps us to frame a superior perspective, which assembles fearlessness, self-respect and a greatly improved picture of self. It is the strategy of social and character headway that is delivered by mind control insider facts.

You would see that the cerebrum has a sustaining side in the event that you understand the brain. This side of the cerebrum rests in the oblivious personality, which licenses us to spoil self.

Down in the profundities of your unceasing personality is the oblivious personality where your mind control privileged insights hang tight for you, which houses the inner self that figures it can control you.

You should turn the light on of your genuine Self and request the personality to adhere to your guidelines.

The mind rests over the oblivious personality. The structure of the oblivious personality you will find common personality control insider facts to advance through social and character improvement in the event that you pursue.

In what way, well, by fathoming your body activities, you can bring the brain and body into congruity. See by the by, that the body simply does precisely what the mind states, so this is the reason it is basic that we create poise.

Intensity of Your Subconscious Mind And Finding Your Purpose in Life

Through the intensity of your intuitive personality you do now and again have glimpses, or a voice, it's a disclosure, maybe, demonstrating to you that you are really a co-maker with God.

We've generally been co-makers with God, however a fantasy of sort, makes them see a different picture with independent characters from God. Thinking about this fantasy of detachment, as it were, can be an incredible right-disapproved of method for taking a gander at the world, and may help you all the more effectively start discovering your motivation throughout everyday life.

Discovering your motivation in life through the intensity of your subliminal personality can be hard to understand.

In our cognizant personality there is significantly more to state about how mankind has turned into the world's visionary. Indeed, we are storytellers.

Through the intensity of your subliminal personality you do now and again have glimpses, or a voice, it's a disclosure, maybe, demonstrating to you that you are genuinely a co-maker with God.

We've generally been co-makers with God, yet a fantasy of sort, makes them see a different picture with independent personalities from God. Mulling over this fantasy of detachment, as it were, can be an extraordinary right-disapproved of method for taking a gander at the world, and may help you all the more effectively start discovering your motivation throughout everyday life.

THIS IS WHAT I MEAN:

At the point when the partition previously happened, a degree of recognition called cognizance turned into a piece of our psyche. An "independent" part, maybe, however illusive. This degree of the cognizant personality made itself a perceiver, as opposed to a maker that is given to you in the intensity of your subliminal personality.

The cognizant personality is the place the sense of self fabricated its space, and we have been making projections, suppositions, and seeing from that point onward.

Our psyches just appear to be longer entire, presently involved by the sense of self - a creative mind of the body being what our identity is, which is a wrong-disapproved of endeavor to see yourself as you wish. The sense of self based cognizant personality causes you to make it hard to tell who you really are.

The personality based personality which is the fanciful part of our mind that thinks, or, we may state dreams it is independent from God the Father, is brimming with inquiries, including how it was made, as opposed to made.

The self-image is great at posing inquiries, however not getting important answers where your actual calling or reason in life concerned. This is along these lines, in light of the fact that any answers would include learning which is of the intensity of your subliminal personality that can't be seen by the inner self.

With this, the cognizant personality ends up befuddled, and discovering your motivation in life can appear to be troublesome, in light of the fact that only One-Mindedness, the intensity of your intuitive personality can be without disarray.

Really, however, by what method can a partitioned and isolated personality not be confounded?

The self-image based personality is dubious about what it is. Being that it is out of accord with itself, it must be in struggle. This makes every single isolated part aliens to one another, and this is the pith of resistance, where assault is readied.

No big surprise we fear our genuine potential that sits in the intensity of your intuitive personality.

With the ongoing strength of the inner self, you have turned out to be frightful of yourself and discovering your motivation in life befuddling, thinking that its difficult to escape from whom you made yourself to be.

Be that as it may, you can, at the present time, at the present time, effectively escape from your misperceptions, suppositions, and anticipated pictures, since they are not valid.

These misperceptions of yourself are mistakes; yet your creation is past blunder, the creation is past the fantasy of partition, and with reality that you are, your part brain can be mended.

We should not mistake right-mindedness for information.

Your right-personality which frequently faculties the intensity of your intuitive personality is just material to right-disapproved of observation, which leads to learning. It's the place you hear that voice about discovering your motivation throughout everyday life. Frequently the voice is faintly heard because of the sense of self's dicey, dreadful, and judgmental gab interrupting.

Right-mindedness when appropriately used is the revision for wrong-mindedness, and is the perspective that overlooks the sense of self and gives you precise discernment as opposed to perplexity. It's the place your inward voice is all the more unmistakably heard.

There will be some uncertainty, yet that is alright, on the grounds that anything not of learning and the intensity of your subliminal personality will without a doubt have its questions.

We can call this marvel disapproved of observation, since supernatural occurrences must be conceivable by the adjusted recognition that starts the recuperating procedure.

Once your observation is befuddled over any issue, huge or little, carry it to the Holy Spirit-your internal Guide Who approaches you from the intensity of your intuitive personality, and after that tune in to His Voice for exact recognition.

Your befuddled recognition will be risen above to a reasonable standpoint of the issue, setting up the basis for a move over to learning.

Venturing to every part of the scaffold over to information need not be a long voyage; frequently it is immediate.

Notwithstanding the time it takes to land at learning from the intensity of your intuitive personality, He will make them see in a constructive and crisp manner similarly as how, with my detainment, I started seeing constructive roads driving me out of jail and into another and compensating life.

Obviously during those 8 long a long time in that unpredictable and regularly brutal commotion of the phone square, I was likewise observing a great deal of negative encounters every day; except I was considering the to be as fuel for the street ahead.

This is the thing that I mean by right-disapproved of observation. It's what you look like at discovering your motivation throughout everyday life.

THE BARRIERS OF MIND

The Problems of Mind can't be understood at the degree of psyche. What are the issues of psyche? Frailty, uneasiness, tension, detachment from the source, a sentiment of segregation, examination, needing for more cash, longing for higher position, status, work and so forth. To finish the LACK or GAP-which is nothing. It just exists in the brain. All things considered we don't need anything. We are superbly made by our maker. These holes and needs are on the whole misrepresentations, ghosts, made by our psyche. They don't exist as a general rule. As a renowned creator has stated:

The moment you realize that you lack nothing; the whole world belongs to you.

Indeed, it is valid. We don't need anything. We needn't bother with a solitary more thing to finish ourselves. At that point from where is this hankering, this need originates from?? Keep in mind; it is all inner self produced. As a matter of fact brain is an instrument of the Ego and needs to make us its instrument. Presently it is up to us. We have two options; either control our brains or get constrained by them. Once we see through the mind commanded focal point, at that point we see needs and holes and wanting and inadequacy all over the place. Psyches gives us a chance to contrast and other individuals of higher status or employment or riches or cash and in a split second our certainty is gone and we are submerged in an ocean of feeling of inadequacy. So we need to leave our psyche, we need to leave our inner self. So what is the arrangement?

In the event that you please allude to the primary line after the inscription it peruses: the problems of mind cannot be solved at the level of mind. I don't get it's meaning?

It implies we need to move one stage up. We need to rise one level over the degree of brain. What's more, what is that? It is no psyche. It implies we need to calm our brain. We need to build up a propensity to tune in to the considerations it ceaselessly produces, as an eyewitness. We need to turn into an onlooker of our considerations. The minutes we just discreetly sit at an agreeable spot and simply watch the considerations that are striking a chord, fair-mindedly; without passing a judgment whether they are correct or wrong, the brain loses its hold on us. We and our mind become two particular substances. We in a split second leave the fantasy that we are our mind. It would be ideal if you note that your mind is different from you. You are a being higher than your psyche. You are a being which can watch, right, control and direct your brain. That is the reason we are called individuals! Psyche is a wonderful instrument when utilized appropriately however once you can't stop the perpetual commotion and musings coming into your head at whatever point you like, at that point realize that the instrument has assumed control over you. It has controlled you. You have turned into its hostage. It has oppressed you!

Presently the inquiry normally emerges how to accomplish this. How to enter this no-mind state at whatever point we like? The appropriate response is present moment. To be a no restriction individual; to be a satisfied individual; to be a finished, tranquil, quiet, balanced, engaged and mollified individual simply live right now. Present minute is an extraordinary danger to mind and to sense of self. Psyche can't stand the present minute. It always takes you either to the past which causes blame and sadness or to the future which causes strain, stress and nervousness. The minute you completely center around the current task, the minute you are completely and totally assimilated in what you are doing directly, it flees. It stows away out of sight and you feel such a delight, tranquility, serenity that can't be communicated in words and must be felt essentially.

Thus, to put it plainly, living right now is the panacea of all issues produced by our mind that are not genuine very rather hinder our advancement, development or more all obliterate our significant serenity.

MIND-BRAIN DUALITY

I have no clue about the legitimacy of the accompanying hypothesis, however I thought I'd simply toss it out into the ether and perceive how it resounds.

Two of the genuine big deal with regards to 1) material science, and 2) nervous system science/brain science are 1) wave - molecule duality, and 2) personality - cerebrum (or body) duality. Could the previous help with clarifying the last mentioned? In the event that particles can transform into waves, can cerebrum matter transform into cerebrum waves and in this way an indication of what we call the brain?

How about we characterize the 'unimportant' or the 'non-physical' as something that falls outside of our typical discernments character- istic in our standard organic tangible contraption. For instance, about the majority of the electromagnetic range (for example - radio waves), attractive fields, ultra-high or low recurrence 'sounds', and so forth. While that may be valid in a restricted sense, it's not so much valid since we presently have mechanical tangible instruments that can recognize what is 'unimportant' or 'non-physical' to our organic tactile instruments. Anyway, by this definition, our brain (or soul, mind, embodiment, character, cognizance, mindfulness, and so on.) is 'insignificant' or 'non-physical' since you can't see, hear, taste, contact or smell your psyche or the brains of others. Your mind lies outside of your standard organic tangible mechanical assembly. So is your mind like radio waves or something different (or nothing else) totally?

Your standard five faculties recognizes whatever parts of reality outer to your mind (that incorporates your body) it can, yet with inalienably work in confinements - your faculties can't distinguish that you are somewhat radioactive for instance. Some portion of what your five standard faculties can't recognize is your brain. However plainly you can identify your psyche, your cognizance, your mindfulness ("I think, hence I am"). In this way, I presume that there must be a type of tangible mechanical assembly inside your cerebrum which distinguishes your mind*. The $64,000 question is what really is the cerebrum's tactile mechanism(s) or structure(s) for detecting or identifying the brain?

In any case, much like your standard five detects, this 'intuition' inalienable inside your cerebrum additionally closes down when you rest. At the point when you rest you have no familiarity with your psyche, no cognizance, no mindfulness, no feeling of self-character, much the same as you have no feeling of slight, of taste, of smell, of sound or of touch under normal conditions (for example - an uproarious applaud of thunder may enroll and wake you up once more into a condition of awareness).

In the event that the cerebrum can recognize the psyche, at that point the brain must be made out of or comprise of a something, though a something that our typical remotely arranged faculties couldn't identify - like radio waves or the body's radioactivity. Presently the cerebrum itself is generally invigorated by the faculties by what are called electro-substance signals or electrical driving forces (for example - particles) and are estimated as 'cerebrum waves' by an electroencephalogram (EEG). There's a transformation between the electro-substance signals or electrical driving forces that is mind action and the subsequent wave nature of the EEG readout dependent on that instrumentation. The EEG instrumentation is a tactile system that identifies cerebrum movement. So there's no doubt for this situation of the comparing molecule to-wave nature. Presently does the cerebrum give its very own natural or neurological instrumentation to recognize the very waves it must deliver or make if the wave - molecule duality intrinsic in quantum material science is right? Well since your cerebrum identifies your psyche, the appropriate response should plainly be "yes".

Be that as it may, are these cerebrum waves indications of what we call appearances of the psyche? You show cerebrum waves day in and day out/52 - in any event, when you rest - however then too your psyche needs to exist in any event, when you rest regardless of whether you're not mindful of it since you have attention to a brain before you rest and following you wake up from rest. Once you display no 'mind waves' then you are clinically dead.

So is the mind a wave marvel likened to water waves or weight waves (for example - sound) or electromagnetic waves? Because a wave is a something doesn't imply that all waves can be distinguished by the organic tangible mechanical assembly we as a whole have, thus those waves we can't recognize we can mark as 'insignificant' or 'non-physical' (for example - radio waves) and we've just noted you can't identify the psyche with our five detects. Be that as it may, the mind can both identify waves and radiate waves since the cerebrum's electro-compound sign or electrical driving forces are particles and we as a whole think about wave - molecule duality.

With the majority of the various electro-substance signals or electrical motivation exercises going on in the mind, all delivering cerebrum rushes of some sort, will undoubtedly get bunches of wave-impedance designs. Theory: varying wave-obstruction examples relate to contrasting mental (personality) expresses no two of which are ever completely indistinguishable. Like the indicator screen in the quantum twofold cut examination, your cerebrum is the finder and can decipher what these regularly evolving wave-impedance examples connote and along these lines you realize what express your brain is in.

So do we have a parallel between psyche - cerebrum duality and wave - molecule duality? The cerebrum comprises of the particles; the mind comprises of the waves. In any case, what kind of waves (and related wavelengths/frequencies)? The appropriate response most likely is inside the domain of electromagnetic waves.

So electro-substance and electrical motivation particles a vital part of cerebrum action can show itself as wave (mind wave) action and some particular structure(s) in the mind can identify these waves (like your eyes can distinguish obvious light waves) and convert and gather them once more into electrical sign which your mind translates as the mind simply like different pieces of your mind recognizes locate by means of your eyes and optic nerve (though I'm certain that is a monstrous distortion).

The change of electro-substance and electrical motivation particles to waves occurs obviously everywhere throughout the body yet there's no wave detector(s) in the non-cerebrum parts of your body to enroll and decipher them. Hence the psyche is simply connected with the cerebrum and not state with the liver or even the heart (in spite of parts and bunches of folklore despite what might be expected). The heart just siphons blood - that is it.

One consequence of the majority of this is if a portion of our cerebrum created electromagnetic waves spill outside of our skulls on some uncommon events, at that point by some coincidence, yet very once in a while, others could get on those and obviously the turn around is genuine as well - clairvoyance anybody? Nonetheless, it would be amazingly uncommon simply like you could have a radio that can tune into 10,000 stations, and there happen to be 10,000 stations however just one is communicating. What chances your radio would coincidentally was tuned to simply that solitary station? Further, the standard reverse square law would propose that any mind created wave signals you may communicate would weaken pretty quickly to underneath edge location levels.

*The cerebrum can identify the psyche (accepting you need to separate the two) - yet on the other hand (once you don't wish to separate the two), by what means can the mind recognize the cerebrum when the mind is likewise completing bunches of exercises you (for example - your cerebrum) have definitely no consciousness of by any stretch of the imagination?

REDUCE STRESS: HOW MINDFULNESS CAN HELP, THE SCOURGE OF MODERN LIFE

Odds are, in the event that you are perusing this correct now you approach power, a web association and a cell phone.

You live in the industrialized world and have been influenced by worry sooner or later in your life.

Worry in present day times is unavoidable.

It is the boondocks for stress and nervousness, mirroring the conditions our predecessors looked on the fields of the Savannah hundreds of years prior.

The notice of pressure has discovered its way into ordinary use, young people currently utilize the term to portray rising feelings of anxiety reading for mid-term tests.

In any case, would we say we are pushed or pretending the side effects to caused to notice our battles?

One thing is sure, stress is genuine. However how your body translates it fluctuates from individual to individual.

Truth be told, your resistance for stress is diverse to a prepared Navy Seal officer. However, we would all be able to concur, when pushed past our emphasize point, our wellbeing decreases.

The uplifting news is, we can utilize care to enable us to explore the deluges of pressure and deal with our lives better.

Care means focusing with a specific goal in mind; with reason, right now, and non-judgementally.

It encourages you adapt to life's difficulties by being available and possessing your body with mindfulness. This is as opposed to out of control musings which go through your brain without your cognizant mindfulness.

"Care - the enduring, non-judgmental mindfulness and acknowledgment of experience - prompts mindfulness and to shifts in our points of view that enable us to see plainly what's going on and how we are responding, to react to triggers and injuries with unquestionably progressively receptiveness, and to confront the procedure of essential change with undeniably greater adaptability and resistance," attest creator Linda Graham MFT in, Bouncing Back: Rewiring Your Brain for Maximum Resilience and Well-Being.

HIDING BENEATH SURFACE

Rehearsing care can enable you to lessen pressure since it moves your autonomic sensory system from a focused on state to a quiet state.

As you are understanding this, there are minor anxieties occurring out of sight you are ignorant of, yet your subliminal personality is mindful to.

Stress is deceptive. It hides underneath the surface and strikes when you wouldn't dare hoping anymore, with it collected worry from an earlier time which can spill you the edge.

I compare it to a sequinned pearl neckband, cut at one point and left to disentangle into pieces. Stress has a similar impact making life disintegrate whenever left untreated.

Care can enable you to adapt to the routine examples of reasoning that command your regular day to day existence.

"The act of care - preparing the cerebrum to concentrate and to fortify cognizant mindfulness - enables us to see our molded examples of reaction plainly so we can get unstuck from them when we have to.

Care causes you see the flood of contemplations going through your mind minute to minute.

It is a way to check in with yourself to see what is occurring underneath the outside of your contemplations.

You might be inclined to responding to outside conditions, yet only sometimes set aside the effort to take note of your passionate prosperity. It is frequently past the point of no return when you sense something on the grounds that an enthusiastic emergency has happened.

Your musings can maneuver you into the past, where you re-experience uninviting occasions.

You are absent, yet reviewing a psychological screenplay occurred quite a while in the past.

This turns into a stressor since you carry uncertain feelings into your collaborations with others, tainting the excellence of the present minute.

"In any case, whenever you let your considerations, stresses, and stresses direct how you experience this minute, you definitely endure, in light of the fact that you're in strife with the real world, with truth. Instead of hitting the dance floor with life, you're in a wrestling match-and the result of the battle isn't in uncertainty Cutting Out Time for Silence

Care can go far when you commit normal time for quiet.

This is accomplished through contemplation and the sensations made in the body.

Contemplation stays your brain to the present minute, so you become mindful to your present minute experience.

It is significant not to battle your considerations or add an analysis to what you feel, however enable yourself to associate with your sentiments.

As you become happy with sitting peacefully, you may wish to cutting edge your training through organized contemplation. This is perfect to reinforce your insight and bring you into a more profound thoughtful state.

The advantages of reflection enable you to isolate from your musings. You become a quiet observer and less put resources into the surge of movement made in the brain.

You are less receptive in light of the fact that you interface with what is occurring before you.

Stress proliferates on the grounds that individuals accept their considerations.

Along these lines, in the event that you are driving home after an antagonistic experience with your chief or associate, and an impolite driver cuts you off in rush hour gridlock, you offer them some appropriately harsh criticism.

However, by rehearsing care you become sensitive to the physical impressions of displeasure before you fight back since you are aware of your passionate state.

Careful mindfulness - watching and reflecting - enables us to step over from the experience existing apart from everything else and watch it from a bigger field of mindfulness that isn't any of those encounters, that is bigger than any of those examples. With that mindfulness, we can start to see various conceivable outcomes for reacting.

Care positively affects your connections. Your enthusiastic prosperity is improved, rather than surrendering to outside upgrades.

The accomplishment of care based pressure decrease lies in

noticing your contemplations non-judgmentally, through the eyes of composure and sympathy.

In doing as such, you perceive considerations go through the scene of your psyche and they needn't transform into negative feelings.

We are vigorously put resources into our contemplations and have an antagonism inclination when tested. This is a developmental instrument to enable us to comprehend our condition.

Along these lines, when musings, emotions or sensations rise, don't overlook them or stifle them, nor dissect or judge them.

Note them as they happen and watch them deliberately however non-judgmentally, minute by minute, in your field of mindfulness.

In the event that your mind meanders state to yourself, "meandering" and take your psyche back to the present minute.

In the event that you wish to be glad and carry on with a tranquil life, be aware of your musings before they lead you down a dangerous way.

Upsetting contemplations are not the wellspring of your bliss, however a result of oblivious deduction left to run wild.

Care causes you to lessen pressure since it grapples you to the present minute where your body occupies.

All things considered, if your body is available doesn't it bode well that your psyche additionally be at this very moment?

CARE: YOUR LINK TO THE UNIVERSE

Care is the mystery of life. An actual existence lived carefully is a real existence lived brimming with harmony, peacefulness, happiness, rapture, delight and sympathy. Care is our immediate connect to the Universe. The arrangement we as individuals have been looking for outside ourselves since the start of current occasions. The basic routine with regards to care has been around for a large number of years; anyway most individuals dispose of this way to deal with life and rather scan for increasingly perplexing and scholarly ways of thinking or procedures. Sadly, this outer adventure never settle itself. There are numerous people and messages accessible that additionally confuse and over examine care. It appears that our sense of self is customized to entangle even the easiest arrangements. Care is intended to be basic, yet a significant method to live. This present focused arrangement enables us to live bona fide lives.

All in all, what precisely is care and how would you apply it to your life? Care is a particular type of reflection or essentially put consciousness existing apart from everything else. There are a wide range of types of reflection, anyway we are going to explicitly concentrate on care contemplation, which this creator accept to be the most down to earth and unadulterated thoughtful exercise. Care includes straightforwardly partaking in every minute as it happens with complete consciousness of your present involvement. Life possibly exists in the Here and Now when rehearsing care. The minute we experience is unadulterated and unadulterated. Care is a "living" reflection that you can rehearse each second of your valuable life. There is no compelling reason to get away to a disconnected spot, as you can take part in care anyplace and at whenever, regardless of what's going on around you.

Rather than giving the peruser one unbending meaning of care, a couple yet compact definitions will be exhibited beneath drawn from the astuteness of different specialists and professionals of care.

Care frees us from recollections of the past and dreams of things to come by bringing truth of the present minute plainly into core interest. They additionally express that care makes us mindful of life's regular supernatural occurrences.

In one of the antiquated Buddhist critiques, it is expressed that care is good judgment, mindfulness to the present.

Contemplation educator expresses that care is having the mindful, adjusted acknowledgment of present involvement. It isn't more convoluted than that. It is opening to or getting the present minute, wonderful or undesirable, similarly all things considered, without either sticking to or dismissing it.

These basic yet significant utilize different articulation and wording, however what they all offer in like manner is that care is by and large totally and completely present forever. It is monitoring what is happening inside and around you in every snapshot of your marvelous presence. We basically practice mindfulness without judgment, tolerating our musings and feelings precisely as they seem to be.

As you may have seen care is a straightforward yet, ground-breaking approach to live our lives. Its essentially being Right Here, Right Now: submerging your general existence right now and completely encountering your life. That is it! It truly is that straight forward. It isn't important to over investigate, intellectualize, or confound what it is to be careful. Obviously our self image needs to occupy us in any capacity conceivable, however don't permit this. Perceive the nearness of your inner self, make proper acquaintance, and afterward tranquilly expel it. Everything to being careful is to Simply Be. While there are bounty further developed clarifications on this theme accessible for you to further investigate once you want; what has been portrayed here is the straightforward and unadulterated substance of care reflection.

As you leave this book and proceed with your adventure of careful living or in the event that you are simply starting, this essayist proposes that you plunge into the sea of Now and personally familiarize yourself with the delight of what is straightforwardly before you. As communicated in the Zen custom, "When eating, estimated time of arrival and when strolling, walk."

YOUR SUBCONSCIOUS MIND IS YOUR PARTNER IN SUCCESS , YOUR BRAIN IS A RECOVERY AND CAPACITY ASSET.

Its job is to understand the present and future while recalling the past. For a few, remembering their youth as grown-ups is very normal. One need just look to the male species to see them carry on like kids seeing someone. They do not have the attention to settle on reasonable choices on occasion and are blinded by basic inclinations.

· · ·

The female species don't get off so gently. A few ladies pick an inappropriate accomplice frequently, in light of the fact that they clutch uncertain youth issues which impede discovering bliss. We as a whole convey awkward agony from early youth, yet when these torment focuses rise we are helpless before our oblivious musings.

An intuitive personality which has eradicated the old negatives and supplanted them with new positives is the most prolific ground for development and accomplishment we will ever discover.

I wish to plot two techniques for arousing your psyche mind's potential for progress.

To work with the subliminal personality, it's imperative to acknowledge how your condition impacts your considerations. For instance, when heading to work think about why Adele's melody Hello sneaks in to your mind later that evening? This is on the grounds that your intuitive personality is mindful to your surroundings which incorporate the verses of the melody.

The intuitive personality is affected by redundancy and boosts. To know and conscious to your surroundings is basic for progress.

Therefore, be aware of the music you tune in to, the TV programs you watch, the individuals you invest your energy with and the material you read, if achievement is your objective.

Individuals are perplexed why they rehash the equivalent ruinous examples seeing someone. They carry on youth practices or unknowingly get negative attributes from past connections. Like an infection, it contaminates your intuitive personality to accept control of your conduct in future connections.

Things being what they are, how can one prepare mind for progress? There are numerous strategies accessible, however I wish to concentrate on a couple that are powerful:

Guided Imagery: Guided symbolism is grounded in utilizing your visual faculties to envision a circumstance, while in a casual state. It's essential to picture the objective or assignment as genuine, while approaching different faculties. Your subliminal personality can't recognize an envisioned state and a genuine one. For instance, when you consider an individual an impolite name, your subliminal personality translates the affront as self-coordinated.

In spite of having the option to translate an abundance of data, the mind needs fitness in separation. This is because of the subliminal personality not testing musings got by the cognizant personality. The cognizant personality forms contemplations while the subliminal personality takes a secondary lounge all the while. Addressing and investigating is the space of the cognizant or logical personality. The psyche mind's errand is to get orders started by the cognizant personality.

Visioning urges receptiveness to special and innovative arrangements. As you hold your plainly characterized vision, the approaches to make that vision happen become clear. Your subliminal personality chips away at your benefit to spot potential chances, prospects, and conceivable outcomes you may some way or another have missed.

Alright, how about we begin on a speedy exercise. Locate an agreeable situated situation, since this enables you to keep up open channels inside the body and you're more averse to nod off in this position.

Take a couple of full breaths to actuate your parasympathetic sensory system (rest and overview framework), which flag the body to unwind. Take in through your nose and breathe out through your mouth. Envision an objective or achievement you wish to attempt. Once its weight reduction or to be in an adoring relationship, envision yourself having accomplished this objective.

What's it like? What are you doing in the scene? Where are you? Imagine the picture admirably well. Are there sounds? Would you be able to get a feeling of smell or taste? Try not to envision something you're reluctant to acknowledge. Enable your intuitive personality to control you through the psychological practice. Once you don't see pictures, attempt again later. I like to tune in to hints of waves slamming or downpour falling before practicing guided symbolism. It enables me to get into an agreeable intuitive learning state.

Guided symbolism requires control and practice, so slide your way into it. Try not to progress too rapidly, since you'll wind up baffled with the training. Analysis and note the pictures that rise. Note their force and the related feelings that emerge. Guided Imagery is figuring out how to associate personality and body while getting to be aware of the vibes that emerge.

Confirmations Before Sleep: The subsequent method is utilizing certifications before rest. Preceding nodding off, your intuitive personality is generally receptive. This is on the grounds that the cognizant personality winds up fatigued handling considerations and is more averse to challenge the confirmations. In case you're prone to break down contemplations before rest, take a stab at reflecting for a brief period. This should help facilitate a fomented personality.

Maybe you didn't understand that each and every time you state "I AM" in a sentence, you are at the same time sending an immediate request and an affirmation to your cerebrum precisely how you genuinely feel about yourself and what you anticipate. You are really sending a direction to your subliminal personality and telling each cell of your body how to react.

Form the certifications you mean to utilize. A very much formed content is the way to successful certifications. Be mindful to your words, all things considered if it's rehashed frequently they should impact you. They should be confirmed, rather than latent: "I am currently my optimal weight" or "I cherish and value my fit, fit and solid body." Wording is fundamental provided that they are obscure, your mind will think that its hard to acknowledge. Consider the expressions of the Adele melody that overflowed your intuitive personality while driving home prior. Melody verses, blended with the correct music, can impact your brain thus too with attestations.

In what capacity will you realize they are the correct confirmations? When presenting them, note the sensations in your body. Is there pressure? It is safe to say that you are mindful of specific feelings that transmit from your chest or somewhere else? This is a sign the certifications are appropriate, in light of the fact that your body is your subliminal personality, as indicated by the late neuroscientist Candace Pert.

We have an approach to give new bearings to our intuitive personalities by conversing with ourselves in an alternate manner, intentionally reconstructing our inside control focuses with words and explanations which are progressively viable, increasingly supportive to all aspects of us that we might want to improve.

Pick a few assertions in any case, as more will include submitting them to memory. We are attempting to put forth our aims for the intuitive personality, not submit words to memory. Rehash the assertions as you float to rest, during the Hypnagogia stage. This is the temporary stage among attentiveness and rest where you are languid. Keep on rehashing the confirmations until you capitulate to tiredness.

So, try different things with the methods to locate the one that works for you. I recommend you read books and take courses to enable you to propel your insight. Once you surrender following a little while in light of the fact that you think that its exhausting or troublesome, you'll neglect to yield long haul gains. It requires time and persistence to get results. You're preparing your mind, like practicing which requires responsibility and devotion.

LIFE AND THE MIND: THROUGH THE WORMHOLE, SEVEN DAYS BY-WEEK OUTLINE OF THE PROGRAM

Week One causes you to see the programmed pilot at work and urges you to investigate what happens when you "wake up." Central to this week is a Body and Breath reflection that balances out the psyche and encourages you to perceive what unfurls when you center your full mindfulness around only each thing in turn. Another shorter reflection encourages you to reconnect with your faculties through careful eating. Albeit the two practices are exceptionally basic, they likewise give the fundamental establishments on which the various reflections are assembled.

Week Two uses a basic Body Scan contemplation to help investigate the contrast between pondering a sensation and encountering it. A significant number of us invest such a large amount of our energy living "in our minds" that we nearly disregard the world experienced straightforwardly through our faculties. The Body Scan contemplation prepares your brain so you can concentrate straightforwardly on your real sensations without judging or breaking down what you find. This causes you to see, always plainly, when the brain has started to meander away without anyone else, so you bit by bit figure out how to "taste" the contrast between the "thinking mind" and the "detecting mind."

Week Three expands on the past sessions with some nonstrenuous Mindful Movement practices dependent on yoga. The developments, despite the fact that they are not troublesome in themselves, enable you to see all the more unmistakably what your psychological and physical breaking points are, and how you respond when you contact them. They help the brain to proceed with the way toward reintegrating with the body. You'll bit by bit discover that the body is impeccably touchy to rising disrupting emotions when you are winding up too objective centered — and this enables you to perceive how tense, irate or despondent you become when things don't turn out the manner in which you need. It's an early cautioning arrangement of significant power and essentialness that enables you to take off issues before they increase relentless energy.

Week Four presents a Sounds and Thoughts reflection that logically uncovers how you can be sucked accidentally into "overthinking." You'll figure out how to consider your to be as mental occasions that come and go simply like sounds. By ruminating over the sounds around you, you'll come to discover that "the psyche is to thought what the ear is to sound." This encourages you to take a "decentered" position to your contemplations and sentiments, seeing them go back and forth in the space of mindfulness. This will upgrade lucidity of mindfulness and urge you to take an alternate point of view on your hecticness and issues.

Week Five presents a contemplation—Exploring Difficulty—that causes you to confront (as opposed to dodge) the troubles that emerge in your life every once in a while. A significant number of life's issues can be left to determine themselves, however some should be looked with a soul of transparency, interest and empathy. Once you don't grasp such troubles, at that point they can progressively curse your life.

Week Six builds up this procedure significantly further, investigating how negative perspectives step by step disperse when you effectively develop adoring consideration and empathy through a Befriending Meditation and demonstrations of liberality in every day life. Developing fellowship towards yourself, including for what you see as your "disappointments" and "deficiencies," is the foundation of discovering harmony in an unhinged world.

Week Seven investigates the nearby association between our day by day schedules, exercises, conduct and mind-sets. At the point when we are pushed and depleted, we regularly surrender the things that "sustain" us to set aside a few minutes for the more "squeezing" and "significant" things. We attempt to get ready. Week Seven spotlights on utilizing contemplation to enable you to settle on progressively dexterous decisions, with the goal that you can accomplish a greater amount of the things that sustain you, and farthest point the drawbacks of those things that channel and exhaust your internal assets. This will assist you with entering a highminded circle that prompts more prominent inventiveness, flexibility and the capacity to appreciate life precipitously for what it's worth, as opposed to how you want it to be. Tensions, stresses and stresses will in any case come, yet they are bound to soften away as you figure out how to meet them with thoughtfulness.

Week Eight causes you to mesh care into your day by day life, with the goal that it's consistently there when you need it the most. The staying a month of the program expand on this work, giving you increasingly down to earth approaches to consider musings to be mental occasions —like mists in the sky—and helping you to develop a frame of mind of acknowledgment, sympathy and compassion toward yourself as well as other people. Furthermore, from this perspective, all else pursues. During the two months of the program we purposely place each component of the careful Being mode in the closer view, so you adapt dynamically, at the most profound of levels, what happens when you wake up to your life. Despite the fact that it appears as though every week is showing an alternate part of care, they are, truth be told, all interrelated. As it has been said that a move in one measurement realizes a move in the others too. This is the reason you will be welcome to do a wide range of practices and to endure with every one for at any rate seven days—for every one of them gives an alternate entryway into mindfulness, and nobody can say which, for you, now in your life, will be most useful in helping you reconnect with what is most profound and savvies inside you.

An expression of alert Before you start, it's imperative to realize that as you travel through the program there will be innumerable events when you'll feel like you've fizzled. Your mind will won't settle. It will race off like a greyhound after a bunny. Regardless of what you attempt, inside seconds your psyche may turn into a cauldron of foaming contemplations. It might feel like you are wrestling a snake. You may even need to place your head in your grasp in misery at regularly accomplishing a quiet perspective. Or on the other hand you may feel languid, and a profound tiredness will start undermining your expectation to remain conscious. You may wind up deduction, nothing is working for me. Be that as it may, these minutes are not indications of disappointment. They are significantly significant. Like having a go at anything new, regardless of whether it's figuring out how to paint or to move, it very well may baffle when the outcomes don't relate to the image you have in your psyche. In these minutes, it pays to persevere with duty and consideration toward yourself. Evident "disappointments" are the place you will get familiar with the most. The demonstration of "seeing" that your psyche has dashed off, or that you are eager or sluggish, is a snapshot of extraordinary learning. You are coming to comprehend a significant truth: that your brain has its very own psyche and that a body has needs that a considerable lot of us disregard for a really long time.

You will step by step come to discover that your musings are not you —you don't need to think about them so literally. You can just watch these perspectives as they emerge, remain some time, and afterward break down. It's enormously freeing to understand that your considerations are not "genuine" or "reality." They are essentially mental occasions. They are not "you." At the exact second when you understand this, the examples of considerations and emotions that held you may abruptly lose energy and enable the psyche to settle. A profound sentiment of happiness may fill your body. Yet, very soon your mind will race off once more.

Inevitably, you will indeed wind up mindful that you are thinking, contrasting, judging. You may now feel baffled. You may think: I thought I truly had it at that point—presently I've lost it ... once more, you will understand that your brain resembles the ocean. It is rarely still. Its waves ascend and down. Your brain may then by and by settle ... in any event for some time. Continuously, the times of quiet serenity will extend and the time it takes for you to understand that your psyche has hustled off will abbreviate. Indeed, even the failure can be perceived as another perspective. Here now, at that point gone ...

In the event that you are completely mindful, at that point you keep up more noteworthy control of your programmed pilot and can utilize it to convey propensities as you need them. For instance, come 5:30 p.m. you may take part in the "end-of-the workday" propensities, for example, a last browse of your messages, shutting down the PC and a fast scrounge through your pack to guarantee that you have your keys, telephone and wallet or tote. Simultaneously, you may proceed with a fascinating discussion with an associate, while contemplating what to have for supper. Be that as it may, you can without much of a stretch lose cognizant control of your programmed pilot. One propensity can wind up setting off the following, which triggers the following ... and the following. For instance, you may return home after work habitually and neglect to meet a companion for a beverage. In such a large number of apparently little ways, propensities can, secretly, assume responsibility for your life. As the years pass, this can turn into a tremendous issue as you surrender increasingly more control of your life to the autopilot —including a lot of what you think. Propensities trigger contemplations, which trigger more musings, which wind up activating yet progressively constant considerations. Parts of negative contemplations and sentiments can shape themselves into examples that intensify your feelings. Before you know it, you can move toward becoming overpowered by profound situated burdens, tensions and sadnesses. What's more, when you've seen the undesirable musings and emotions, they'll have turned out to be too solid to even think about containing. A "negligent" remark by a companion can leave you feeling miserable and shaky.

A driver who cuts before you can spill you the edge into fractiousness and outrage. You can be left feeling depleted, frenzied and skeptically separated from the world. At that point you may feel regretful about your loss of control. Another bit of the descending winding has started ... You may frantically attempt and take off the winding of worry by attempting to smother it. You may have a go at contending with yourself, letting yourself know: I'm inept for feeling like this. Be that as it may, such contemplating musings, sentiments and feelings basically aggravates them. Very soon the autopilot can end up overburden with such a large number of considerations, recollections, nerves and errands—simply like a PC with an excessive number of windows left open. Your brain backs off. You may end up depleted, on edge, rushed and incessantly disappointed with life.

Also, once more, much the same as a PC, you may solidify—or even crash. At the point when you arrive at the point where such over-burden has seized up the cognizant personality, it's extremely hard to turn around the procedure essentially by considering your way, for this resembles opening one more program on the PC, over-layering it with one more window. Rather, you have to discover a method for venturing outside the cycle nearly when you see it's started. This is the initial phase in figuring out how to manage life all the more skillfully. It includes preparing yourself to see when your autopilot is dominating, with the goal that you would then be able to settle on a decision about what you need your brain to center upon. You have to figure out how to shut down a portion of the "programs" that have been left running out of sight of your psyche.

The primary phase of recovering your natural care includes coming back to fundamentals. You have to relearn how to concentrate your mindfulness on each thing in turn. Do you recall the Chocolate contemplation from Chapter Three (see p. 55)? Presently you can investigate this further by doing a comparable exercise in careful eating. The Raisin reflection (inverse page) is a progressively unpretentious rendition of eating chocolate carefully. You may locate that giving extremely close consideration to what you're eating will change the involvement in very surprising manners. You just need do this training once, however you can clearly do it the same number of times as you wish. It's a sampler, in a manner of speaking. After you've done it, you have begun the care reflection program.

THE RAISING MEDITATION

DECLINE YOUR TENSION SIDE EFFECTS

Set aside five to ten minutes when you can be separated from everyone else, in a spot, and at once, when you won't be upset by the telephone, family or companions. Switch off your phone, so it doesn't play at the forefront of your thoughts. You will require a couple of raisins (or other dried organic product or little nuts). You'll likewise require a bit of book and a pen to record your responses a while later. Your errand will be to eat the natural product or nuts in a careful manner, much as you ate the chocolate before. Peruse the guidelines beneath to get a thought of what's required, and possibly rehash them in the event that you truly need to. The soul where you do the contemplation is a higher priority than covering each guidance in moment detail. You ought to spend around twenty to thirty seconds on every one of the accompanying eight phases:

1. Holding Take one of the raisins (or your decision of dried natural product or nuts) and hold it in the palm of your hand, or between your fingers and thumb. Concentrating on it, approach it as though you have never observed anything like it. Would you be able to feel the heaviness of it in your grasp? Is it throwing a shadow on your palm?

2. Seeing Take the time truly to see the raisin. Envision you have never observed one. Take a gander at it with extraordinary consideration and complete consideration. Give your eyes a chance to investigate all aspects of it. Inspect the features where the light sparkles; the darker hollows, the folds and edges.

3. Contacting Turn the raisin over between your fingers, investigating its surface. How can it feel between the pointer and thumb of the other hand?

. Smelling Now, holding it underneath your nose, see what you see with each in-breath. Does it have an aroma? Give it a chance to fill your mindfulness. What's more, if there is no fragrance, or practically nothing, see this also.

5. Putting Slowly take the item to your mouth and notice how your hand and arm know precisely where to put it. And after that delicately place it in your mouth, seeing what the tongue does to "get" it. Without biting, just investigate the impressions of having it on your tongue. Bit by bit start to investigate the item with your tongue, proceeding for thirty seconds or more in the event that you pick.

6. Biting When you're prepared, deliberately bring a chomp into the raisin and notice the impacts on the book, and in your mouth. Notice any preferences that it discharges. Feel the surface as your teeth nibble into it. Proceed with gradually biting it, however don't swallow it presently. Notice what's going on in the mouth.

7. Gulping See in the event that you can identify the principal expectation to swallow as it emerges in your brain, encountering it with full mindfulness before you really swallow. Notice what the tongue does to set it up for gulping. Check whether you can pursue the vibes of gulping the raisin. Once you can, deliberately sense it as it descends into your stomach. What's more, once you don't swallow everything at once, intentionally see a second or even a third swallow, until it has all gone. Notice what the tongue does after you have gulped.

8. Eventual outcomes finally, put in almost no time enrolling the consequence of this eating. Is there a persistent flavor? What does the nonappearance of the raisin feel like? Is there a programmed propen-

sity to search for another? Presently bring a minute to record whatever you saw when you were doing the training.